The Mystery
Trivia
Quiz Book

The Mystery Trivia
Quiz Book

by
Kitty Reese
and Regis Sinclair

BELL PUBLISHING COMPANY
New York

For Willy and the cherubs.
—K.R.

For the School of the King.
—R.H.S.

Acknowledgments

Special thanks go to Jean Hazel for her help in the typing of the manuscript, Allen C. Kupfer, Rick Meyers, and Donna Benedetto, for their helpful suggestions and research, and of course all of our friends at Warner Books who made this book possible.

Special thanks also go to all mystery writers both past and present because without them this would have been a very short volume indeed.

This 1985 edition is published by Bell Publishing Company, distributed by Crown Publishers, Inc., by arrangement with Warner Books.

Printed and bound in the United States of America

Library of Congress Cataloging in Publication Data

Reese, Kitty.
  The mystery trivia quiz book.

  1. Detectives and mass media—Miscellanea.
I. Sinclair, Regis. II. Title.
P96.D4R43 1985   809.3′872   85-11217
ISBN 0-517-476746

h g f e d c b a

Contents

Introduction

The seminal part of a mystery is without a doubt the puzzle. Though exotic locales, complex and personable characters, and acts of the grotesque and the perverse add to the genre's popular appeal, it is the recognition of the mystery's inherent puzzle and solution that literally make a mystery a mystery.

The puzzle can obviously take many different forms: the who, what, when and where of a murder, the enigmatic absence of apparent clues at the scene of a crime, and the significance of a long forgotten act from some character's shadowy past. In each case the reader as investigator must evaluate the situation and attempt to draw from it a meaningful solution.

In some cases a puzzle may be impossible to solve without some sort of deus ex machina manipulation by the author. Many times this takes the form of a character's lapse of memory, hidden past, or well-guarded secret. In such cases it is the other characters' memories that are important because it is within these memories of the past (even if they are not recorded in the text proper) that the keystone of the puzzle will become apparent.

As longtime mystery fans we are more than aware of the importance of a good memory, and have with this book attempted to compose a test of your memory for the minor details of some of our favorite mysteries for your pleasure and amusement. The subject matter that we have chosen is obviously based on our own personal favorites and is in no sense meant to be either all inclusive or critically discriminatory. There will always be classics and personal favorites that have been left out, and we hope to someday have the opportunity to fill in some of our gaps wtih a subsequent volume of mystery minutiae.

We wrote this book as fans of the genre and by no means consider ourselves as master authorities, or kings of the realm. We have enjoyed the writing of this little project, and only hope that our readers will too.

Now do you remember...

The Mystery Trivia Quiz Book

Humble Origins

The mystery genre did not begin with the likes of Sherlock Holmes of Baker Street or some down-on-his-luck private investigator of L.A. Elements of mystery have been incorporated into novels since their original conception ... and in some cases even before the novel ever existed.

In Sophocles's *Oedipus Rex,* Oedipus must find the murderer of the previous king of Thebes and bring him to justice to end the plague that has been terrorizing his kingdom.

1. Who was the murderer of the previous king of Thebes?

"The *Oresteia* trilogy" of Aeschylus also dealt with the subject of regicide.

2. Who was the murdered king?

3. Who were the murderers?

Shakespeare's most famous tragedies frequently involve ambition, murder, and deception.

4. Who was the killer of Hamlet's father?

5. What method did the killer use?

6. Who does Macbeth kill to become king?

7. How many murders take place in *Richard III*?

A key element of the plot of Henry Fielding's *Tom Jones* (1749) is the question of Tom's parentage.

8. Who is Tom's real mother?

***Caleb Williams* (1794) by William Godwin concerns the theme of the individual and the social consequences crime, utilizing a very early example of the concept of "being framed."**

9. What is the novel's subtitle?

Charles Brockden Brown is considered by many to be the first American novelist. In *Edgar Huntly* (1799), a young man goes in search of the murderer of his fiancé's brother.

10. Who is the murder suspect?

11. In what state of consciousness is he when Huntly discovers his secret?

Edgar Allan Poe, the father of American short fiction, is also the father of the detective story.

12. What is the name of Poe's detective?

13. Where did he live?

14. What story by Poe is considered to be the first locked-room mystery?

15. Which of Poe's mystery stories is based on an actual case?

Emile Gaboriau developed a detective for several of his stories loosely based on the exploits of the legend-

ary French criminal-expert Vidocq. As with Vidocq, the character foresook a life of crime for a career in police work.

16. What is the fictional detective's name?

17. What other famous detective of later years referred to him, unjustifiably, as "a miserable bungler"?

Charles Dickens often used mystery motifs in his elaborately plotted novels.

18. In *Great Expectations* (1861), who is Pip's secret benefactor?

19. What is the name of the detective featured in *Bleak House* (1853)—the first appearance of one in an English novel?

His last novel was *The Mystery of Edwin Drood* (1870) which was left unfinished at the time of his death, thus leaving the mystery unsolved.

20. Who is the alleged murder victim?

21. Who are the novel's two key suspects?

22. What contemporary and personal friend of Dickens wrote a conclusion to the novel that was published with the original work?

Wilkie Collins's *The Moonstone* (1868) has been dubbed by many the first and best detective novel ever written. It involves the disappearance of a sacred and priceless gem, the Moonstone, from a Victorian estate. When the local superintendent fails to find the culprit, a detective from Scotland Yard is called in.

23. What is this detective's name?

24. What is his favorite pastime?

Victor Hugo's *Les Misérables* (1862) has at its focus a single crime from which the novel's action evolves, namely the pursuit of the criminal Jean Valjean by the dogged Inspector Javert.

25. What crime did Valjean commit?

The Leavenworth Case (1878) by Anna Katherine Green is credited with being the first American detective novel.

26. What is the name of the novel's detective?

27. What other claim to fame does *The Leavenworth Case* have?

The Strange Case of Dr. Jekyll and Mr. Hyde (1886) by Robert Louis Stevenson, in addition to its psychological elements, contains more than a few elements of the modern detective story.

28. By what method does the lawyer Utterson come to the conclusion that there is more than a slight connection between Jekyll and Hyde?

29. Who does Edward Hyde murder, thus forcing him to go into hiding?

Sir Arthur Conan Doyle's brother-in-law, E. W. Hornung, created a character of criminology, only equalled in its contemporary popular appeal by the legendary Sherlock Holmes.

30. What is the name of Hornung's famous rogue?

31. Who narrates his adventures?

The mystery in Mark Twain's *Pudd'nhead Wilson* (1894) involves the switching of a slave's son with the master's child.

32. What revolutionary new techniques of detection were used to establish their true identities?

Maurice LeBlanc, a police reporter for a French newspaper, created a famous fictional character of the French underworld known as the Prince of Thieves.

33. What was this character's name?

Arthur Melville Davisson Post was a lawyer before turning his pen to the mystery genre at the turn of the century. Perhaps his most famous creation is a homespun detective of the Virginia mountain country.

34. By what name is this folksy shamus known?

Before there was ever a Nero Wolfe, there was M. P. Shiel's Prince Zaleski, a pre–Bolshevik Russian nobleman-in-exile who solved mysteries from his couch through sheer concentration.

35. What was his major vice?

Baroness Orczy, author of *The Scarlet Pimpernel*, also wrote numerous mystery stories featuring a strange old man who resided at a certain table in a local tea shop and an impetuous young female reporter.

36. What was the old man usually referred to as?

37. What was the young reporter's name?

38. For what paper did she write?

R. Austin Freeman's Doctor John Thorndyke was introduced in *The Red Thumb Mark* (1907). As both a barrister and a doctor, he was the perfect synthesis of the man of science and the man of letters.

39. What are the names of his two assistants/colleagues?
40. What was his address?

Sir Arthur Conan Doyle

Sir Arthur Conan Doyle cultivated his keen powers of observation and deductive reasoning through his early study and instruction in medicine. Dr. Joseph Bell, a diagnostician and an old teacher of Doyle's, taught him how to best analyze and memorize little details that would be important in his studies. No small wonder that Dr. Bell would be the model for Sherlock Holmes.

1. Name the magazine that originally published "A Study in Scarlet" (1887).

2. Doyle's childhood hero was a character from Edgar Allan Poe's stories. Identify the character.

3. Where did Doyle get material to write "Stark Munro's Letters" and "The Captain of Polestor"?

4. Which one of Doyle's books earned him a knighthood in 1902?

5. To what unit was Watson attached during the second Afghan War?

6. During what battle was he wounded?

7. What was the name of Watson's first wife?

8. What is Holmes's landlady's full name?

9. How is Holmes related to the Danish explorer Sigerson?

10. How much younger is Sherlock than his brother Mycroft?

11. Who did Holmes dub "*the* woman"?

12. What is the name of the noted mathematical paper written by Professor Moriarty?

13. What were the only two cases narrated by Holmes himself?

14. Where did Holmes meet Moriarty in a battle to the death?

"A Study in Scarlet" published in 1887 was the beginning of the friendship between Sherlock Holmes and Dr. Watson and just one of the many cases in which Scotland Yard sought help from the Great Detective.

15. Where was Sherlock Holmes employed when Dr. Watson first met him?

16. As the police moved the dead man's body what fell to the floor?

17. What was the meaning of the word "RACHE," written in blood on the dining room wall?

18. What countersign did Jefferson Hope give the Mormon sentinel?

19. Name the two officials that Holmes helped out at Scotland Yard.

The Adventures of Sherlock Holmes **were a series of short stories, published in the** *Strand Magazine* **between July, 1891 and June, 1892. The Great Detective and** his cohort Dr. Watson have been universally popular with all amateur armchair detectives ever since.

"A Case of Identity"

20. Where did Miss Mary Sutherland and Mr. Hosmer Angel meet?

21. Identify the foreman of Mr. Sutherland's plumbing business.

"The Adventure of the Noble Bachelor"

22. Hatty Doran had a maid. What was her name?

23. What did Hatty drop in front of Frank Moulton at the church?

24. Who caused a big commotion at Mr. Doran's house after the wedding?

The Memoirs of Sherlock Holmes ("Strand Magazine," December 1892–December 1893)

"The *Gloria Scott*"

25. What did seaman Hudson use to get a job on Justice of the Peace Trevor's estate?

26. The mutiny of the prisoners on board the *Gloria Scott* was led by whom?

27. Who was James Armitage?

The Return of Sherlock Holmes ("Strand Magazine," October 1903)

"The Adventure of the Empty House"

28. How did Holmes defend himself against Professor Moriarty on the cliff?

29. Who was the only person that knew Holmes wasn't dead?

30. Who did Holmes consider to be the second most dangerous man in London?

The Hound of the Baskervilles (1902)

31. Where did Sir Charles Baskerville make his fortune?

32. How did Rodger Baskerville die?

33. Who owned the walking stick that Holmes and Watson were discussing as the novel begins?

34. Where did Sir Henry Baskerville live most of his early years?

35. What was stolen from Sir Henry upon his arrival in England?

36. What is the name of the bog that borders the Baskerville estate?

37. Who resided at the Merripit House?

The Valley of Fear (1915)

38. What was the name of "the valley of fear"?

39. Where was Jack Douglas thought to have been murdered?

40. Whose body was turned over to the authorities in his place?

Agatha Christie

Agatha Christie was educated privately at home and had studied singing and piano in Paris. She did so well at both that if she hadn't decided to write she could have had a career as a singer or pianist. Early in her career she wrote romantic novels using the pseudonym Mary Westmacott. She garnered material for many stories from the expeditions she went on with her second husband, archaeologist Max Mallowan. According to Christie, she got some of her best ideas while sitting in the bathtub munching on apples. She is a universally popular writer and her books have been translated into numerous languages as well as into plays and films.

In *Postern of Fate* (1973), Tommy and Tuppence Beresford have just moved into "The Laurels," their new home, where they find a child's book containing a coded message suggesting that Mary Jordan had not died a natural death. Their curiosity aroused, they set out to track down the facts and find themselves deeply involved in pursuit of clues that may very well be the death of the two of them.

1. What was "The Laurels" called when Mary Jordon lived there?

2. Name the book the message was found in and the child who owned the book.

3. Who tried to kill Tuppence and Tommy as they searched for clues in the K. K.?

4. What was the K. K.?

5. Where did the Beresfords find the evidence of renewed fascist activities in the area of Swallows Nest?

Poison-pen letters and murder are grist for Agatha Christie's mill. In *The Moving Finger* (1942), Christie is at her tantalizing best as she takes Jerry Burton and his sister Joanna through a rather puzzling time in the quiet little village of Lymstock.

6. What did the first letter to Jerry and Joanna accuse them of?

7. Why did the murderer send the anonymous letters to so many of the villagers?

8. Who was the one person who did not receive a poison-pen letter?

9. Where did the murderer hide the weapons he had used to kill Agnes?

***At Bertram's Hotel* (1965) the owners have restored everything possible back to the days before World War II. All very charming and nostalgic but for Miss Marple's unfailing ability to sense things being not quite right.**

10. Name the racing-car driver who came looking for Elvira Blake.

11. Where was Canon Pennyfeather going when he disappeared?

12. Who really owned Bertram's Hotel?

13. Why did Elvira shoot Michael Gorman?

14. What first made Miss Marple suspect something was wrong at Bertram's?

15. Who was the head of the crime syndicate of which Bertram's was a part?

In *The Sleeping Murder* (1976), Miss Marple's young friends, the Reeds, have just bought an old house only to find that a murder may have been committed there. Miss Marple is at her sleuthing best when she solves a crime that is twenty years old!

16. What did Gwenda Reed find out about the new house after she bought it?

17. Gwenda experienced *déjà-vu* that really frightened her. What was it?

18. Why did the murderer's hands look like smooth monkey's paws?

19. Whose "posh" car was seen outside the house on the night of the murder?

20. Miss Marple recognized something the murderer was quoting from. What was it?

Despite the popularity of such characters as Tuppence and Tommy Beresford and Miss Jane Marple of St. Mary Mead, Christie's most famous character has to be the little Belgian detective Hercule Poirot whose career ran from 1920 to 1975.

Poirot began and ended his career at the same country estate.

21. What was its name?

22. What were the titles of his first and last cases?

In his final case, Poirot reveals his obsession with a murderer whom no court would ever convict, thus forcing him to take on all three roles of judge, jury, and executioner.

23. What is Poirot's name for this murderer, and what is his real name?

24. What are the circumstances of Poirot's death?

The novel that first brought Poirot to critical notoriety was *The Murder of Roger Ackroyd* (1926), which has become recognized as possibly *the* landmark mystery novel of the twentieth century because of its inspired plot twist.

25. What is Poirot doing the first time we see him in the course of the novel?

26. How did Ackroyd die?

27. What was the name of Ackroyd's estate and where was it located?

28. Who killed Roger Ackroyd?

***Murder on the Orient Express* (British title, *Murder in the Calais Coach*) (1934) offers Poirot a captive group of suspects on a stalled train with an extremely limited amount of time to solve a truly baffling murder.**

29. What train does Poirot board at the novel's beginning?

30. Why does he refuse to accept Mr. Ratchett's offer of a job as his bodyguard?

31. What is the telltale message that Poirot is able to derive from a charred paper fragment?

32. What was Ratchett's real identity?

33. In *The ABC Murders* (1936), who are A, B, and C?

34. Who is the next victim in the sequence?

Halloween Party (1969) is one of Poirot's most famous cases to feature another memorable Christie character—Mrs. Ariadne Oliver.

35. What is Ariadne's profession and her obsession?

36. What is the name of the boastful student who is murdered in the tub used in bobbing for apples?

37. Who hosted the Halloween party of the title?

38. What other cases featured both Poirot and Oliver?

39. Who is the recurrent narrator for many of Poirot's cases?

On a lighter note, a Broadway musical of the seventies featured a song called "I Owe It All to Agatha Christie."

40. What was the title of this musical and upon what Christie novel was it loosely based?

Raymond Chandler

After serving in World War I and working for years in the oil industry, Raymond Chandler turned to writing mystery novels at the age of forty-five. With the success of his first novel The Big Sleep *(1939), Chandler wrote six more novels, and such original screenplays as* The Blue Dahlia *(1946) and* Double Indemnity *(1944). His "tough guy" detective, Philip Marlowe, is probably his biggest claim to fame. Chandler died in 1959, the same year he was elected president of the Mystery Writers of America.*

Philip Marlowe is a tough guy but he lets himself get soft when he decides to play the Good Samaritan to a drunk, Terry Lennox, thus winding up involved in murder and deception in *The Long Goodbye* (1953)

1. How much did Sylvia Lennox give Terry Lennox when he remarried her?

2. Where did Mrs. Wade get the pendant she wore around her neck?

3. What name did Terry Lennox use when he married Eileen Wade in 1942?

4. In Eileen's suicide note what confession did she make?

5. Who was Amos?

6. What was the connection between Linda Loring and Sylvia Lennox?

7. The last time Marlowe saw Terry Lennox he was using another alias. What was it?

When Philip Marlowe is hired to find a missing wife things get very complicated—with a cop gone bad, a woman who can mean nothing but trouble, and an old murder case that has been resurrected. It's all in *The Lady in the Lake* (1943).

8. In the telegram that Crystal Kingsley sent her husband who did she say she intended to marry?

9. What was the name of the lake the woman's body was found in?

10. Who did Dr. Almore cover up for when his wife was murdered?

11. Why did Marlowe suspect Degarmo?

12. What was there between Degarmo and Muriel Chess?

13. Who was Derace Kingsley's secretary?

14. Name the hotel where Bird Keppel worked as a beautician.

Philip Marlowe accidentally gets mixed up in a murder and finds his arms filled with plenty of beautiful women in *Farewell My Lovely* **(1940). Usually Marlowe is very happy to have beautiful women around, but this time it's just too hazardous to his health.**

15. Who was the "big man" looking for?

16. Name the club Velma sang in.

17. Marriott took Marlowe to a canyon to kill him but was killed himself instead. What was the name of the canyon?

18. Who helped Marlowe get aboard the *Montecito*?

19. What kind of jade was Mrs. Grayle's necklace made of?

20. Who was Laird Brunette?

John Creasey

John Creasey worked at various clerical jobs before he decided to start writing full-time in 1935. Until his death in 1973, Creasey had written about five hundred and sixty novels using more than twenty different pseudonyms. He was one of the most prolific and popular writers of mysteries in the world. Dr. Palfrey, the Baron, and Inspector West are just a few of Creasey's most interesting characters.

Innocent bystander Neil Banister unwittingly becomes the only person who can help Dr. Palfrey and his force in a situation that is threatening the safety of all living things on Earth in *The Touch of Death* (1954).

1. What discovery was Professor Monk-Gilberts murdered for?

2. Why was Neil Banister so valuable to Dr. Palfrey and Z5?

3. How did Dr. Palfrey meet Neil Banister?

4. Where is "the perfect world" and who was its leader.

5. What was the leader's name that the perfect world?

There's *A Bundle for the Toff* (1967) right on his doorstep. And he brought a lady friend home with him. It looks

17

like someone is out to destroy Richard Rollison's good name, or maybe just steal it!

6. How did the baby arrive on Rollison's doorstep?

7. In what way does Bill Ebbutt help the Toff?

8. Why was Kate McGuire murdered?

9. Who rescued Rollison from the river?

10. What was the name of the criminal who was a threat to the baby and its mother?

In *Stars for the Toff* (1968), the Honorable Richard Rollison reluctantly decides to help a fortune-teller accused of fraud, and ends up needing her second sight to "see" him through the solution of a very puzzling murder case.

11. How did the Toff meet the fortune-teller?

12. Name the fortune-teller.

13. What is Rollison's Black Museum?

14. Why was Mrs. Abbott killed?

15. Who was Syd Bishop?

There's *A Sharp Rise in Crime* (1975) when a gang of thieves start having great success by doubling as very prominent people during their robberies. One of them has even gone so far as to masquerade as Inspector Roger West.

16. What was wrong with the picture of West that was sent to the CID?

17. In his investigation, whose identity does West take to go undercover?

18. Someone from Scotland Yard was working with the gang of thieves. Name him.

19. Where was Inspector West's son Martin supposed to meet him with a camera?

20. A New York policewoman was invaluable to West when he went undercover. What was her name?

Mignon G. Eberhart

Mignon G. Eberhard was born in 1899 in Nebraska and attended Wesleyan University (1917–1920). Her first novel was published in 1929, and her second book won her the Scotland Yard prize. She is recognized among her many readers and fans as the American counterpart to Agatha Christie, and at least six of her books have been made into motion pictures.

In *El Rancho Rio* (1970), Mady Wilson thinks her husband Craig is involved in a murder and she's trying to protect him. Then Craig's sister-in-law is found murdered and the number of suspects increases. Finally Mady, herself in danger, realizes that she should have left the solving of murders to the police.

1. What did Mady Wilson remove from the scene of the murder when she found Casso's body?

2. Where did Mady hide her bloodstained gloves?

3. Edith Wilson had found something that caused her death—what did she find?

4. Who masterminded the scheme to defraud Craig Wilson?

5. Why was Casso murdered?

In *Witness at Large* (1966), Tom Esseven was being charged with murder, but Cornelia was certain he was innocent. So she married him. After all, a wife can refuse to testify against her own husband. She never thought that her marriage would put her in danger of becoming another victim.

6. Who is Egbert Drippley?

7. Why was Mildred murdered?

8. How much money did the Bronsons offer to pay for the business?

9. What did Mrs. Bronson pay Alice to do?

10. Why did Cobwell want Cornelia out of the way?

Rose Manders is the wife of a very wealthy financier in *Danger Money* (1974). She also has numerous relatives who are supported by her rich husband. So when Rose is found murdered, the police have more than enough suspects. Actually, there are just too many!

11. Where was the missing helicopter found?

12. Who did Susan see running away?

13. What was the connection between Ligon Clanser and John Nelson?

14. What finally gave Ligon Clanser away?

15. From what profession had Bert Prowde retired, and what was his nickname?

Drue Cable returned to Brent Hall to nurse her ex-husband Craig Brent back to health after he had been shot. Then Drue's ex-father-in-law is found dead, and Drue finds herself being accused of murder in *Wolf in Man's Clothing* (1942).

16. Drue arrived at Brent Hall with another nurse. Name the other nurse.

17. How did Peter Huber insinuate himself into the Brent home?

18. Why did Conrad Brent shoot his son Craig?

19. The night Conrad Brent died who phoned the police and said it was murder?

20. What connection was there between Anna Haub and Peter Huber?

Dick Francis

Born in Wales in 1920, Dick Francis left school at the age of fifteen "because all I ever wanted to do was ride horses." Before Francis was forced to retire after he had damaged his spleen in an accident, he was one of Britain's leading steeplechase jockeys. It is from this rich background in racing that he is able to write first-rate mystery novels about the world of thoroughbred racing.

In *Reflex* (1981), photographer Philip Nore becomes a target of a killer when he discovers evidence of corruption and blackmail after a racing photographer is killed. To complicate matters for Nore, he must locate the sister, who until now, he never knew he had.

1. In developing the negatives he found in George Millace's rubbish box what did Philip Nore discover?

2. What form of blackmail did Millace use on his victims?

3. Who was it that Nore couldn't prove killed George Millace?

4. Before she died, Philip's grandmother gave him some shocking news. What was it?

5. In what magazine did Philip advertise Amanda's picture?

Sid Halley was a champion jockey until an accident forced him to give up the track. Now he's racing against criminals trying to manipulate thoroughbred racing and a con man who has involved his ex-wife in fraud in *Whip Hand* (1979).

6. What was the strange disease that the afflicted horses suffered from?

7. Who benefited most from the horses becoming diseased?

8. Name the horse expected to be cured of the disease through rare antibiotics.

9. What was the charity that Sid's ex-wife became a fundraiser for?

10. Nicholas Ashe was an alias used by whom?

11. What product were people buying in support of the phony charity?

In *Forfeit* (1969), newspaperman James Tyrone is hired to do a story on the famous Lamplighter race. What he didn't bargain for was involvement in a racing scandal, a very suspicious "accidental" death of a famous sportswriter, and, least of all, falling in love.

12. Before Bert Checkov died he advised Tyrone of two things he should never sell. What were they?

13. What was Checkov forced to write in his column?

14. Where did Tyrone hide the horse Tiddley Pom?

15. Who took over Charlie Boston's string of betting parlors?

Tim Ekaterin enjoys being a banker in the 1982 novel of the same name. He's interested in money and finds it exciting until a credit investigation unfolds into the murder of a young girl and a fraudulent scheme to fix races.

16. Where did Tim first meet Calder Jackson?

17. What was given to the mares that would cause their foals to be deformed?

18. How was it administered to the mares?

19. Who was the pharmacist that helped Tim find the source of the substance?

20. Why was Ginnie Knowles murdered?

Erle Stanley Gardner

As a teenager Erle Stanley Gardner earned money as a boxer. He was admitted to the California Bar in 1911 and began writing mystery stories during the 1920s. He wrote more than sixty novelettes about the adventures of Lester Leith, a kind of Robin Hood of detectives, and in 1933 he gave up practicing law to become a full-time writer. He wrote eighty-two Perry Mason novels and twenty-nine Donald Lam–Bertha Cool mysteries using the pseudonym, A. A. Fair.

The Case of the Postponed Murder (1973) was exactly that. A photograph of Perry Mason's client Mae Farr has some connection with a murder. Perry has to find more than meets the eye if he is going to save her.

1. Who took the incriminating picture of Mae Farr and Penn Wentworth?

2. What was the coinlike object seen in the photograph of Farr and Wentworth?

3. Why did Hazel Tooms kill Penn Wentworth?

4. Name the justice of the peace in the trial.

5. How did Mason prove that Hazel Tooms was guilty?

In *The Case of the Troubled Trustee* (1965), Perry Mason is certain that the only thing his client is guilty of is making a fortune for his ward. But, Desere Ellis wants to donate all her money to a fund for aspiring young artists, and somehow trustee Kerry Dutton is mixed up in murder.

6. Desere Ellis's father left her stock that was considered "a dog," but suddenly was worth a fortune. Name the stock.

7. To whom was Desere giving her money for the foundation to fund young artists?

8. Why was Roger Palmer killed?

9. What evidence did George W. Holbrook give at the trial?

10. Where was the empty .32-caliber brass cartridge-case found?

The All-Purpose Insurance Company wants to pay Donald Lam and Bertha Cool a lot of money to prove that Helmann Bruno is a malingerer. Lam quickly finds that much more than insurance is at stake in *Up For Grabs* (1964).

11. What is the name of the ranch where Bruno wins a vacation?

12. Name the photographer who was staying at the ranch when Homer Breckenridge was there.

13. Who stole a set of X rays for Bruno?

14. How did Lam get in to see Mrs. Bruno?

15. Homer Breckenridge had a connection at the ranch. Who was it?

The relatively simple job of being a bodyguard to the very beautiful Marilyn Chalen soon becomes a very complex case of murder and blackmail for Donald Lam and Bertha Cool in *Fish or Cut Bait* (1965).

16. Who first hired and subsequently fired Lam and Cool as bodyguards to Marilyn Chalen?

17. Who called Mr. Gillett from the motel where Boxter Gillett had just died?

18. What was the connection between George Dix and Hermann Oakley?

19. Sergeant Frank Sellers had a nickname for Donald Lam. What was it?

20. Who was Norman Clinton?

Dashiell Hammett

Dashiell Hammett, veteran of both World Wars, former Pinkerton investigator, and famed companion of Lillian Hellman, has become recognized as the master of the perfect synthesis of the intellectual and hard-boiled genres of detective fiction. His detectives—such as Sam Spade and Nick Charles—have since become American archetypes.

The Continental Op was Hammett's first successful detective character. Though nameless, this investigator for the Continental Detective Agency in San Francisco figured as the main character in numerous stories and in the novels *Red Harvest* (1929) and *The Dain Curse* (1929).

1. In what magazine did the first Continental Op stories appear?

2. What is the name of his boss back at the agency?

3. In *Red Harvest*, what is the name of the town that has been taken over by criminals?

4. What was the name of the Op's client who was killed the first night the Op was on the case?

5. What was his job?

6. What was the town's principle industry?

7. What is meant by the Dain curse?

8. Why is the Op originally called in on the case?

9. What is the name of the bizarre cult that has seemingly seduced the heiress Gabrielle Leggett?

The Maltese Falcon (1930) immediately brings to mind the movie images of Bogart, Greenstreet, Lorre, and the black bird itself. But of course the novel came first.

10. What was Sam Spade's partner's name?

11. What was Casper Gutman's nickname?

12. What was Sam Spade's secretary's name?

13. How does she describe Brigid O'Shaughnessy to Sam?

14. How much does Joel Cairo initially offer Sam for the black bird?

15. How much does Sam put the bite on Gutman for his time and expenses?

The debonair detective Nick Charles only appeared in one novel, The Thin Man (1934), but his legacy lived on in a host of movie sequels.

16. Of what national descent is Nick?

17. For what organization did Nick formerly work?

18. What type of dog was Asta?

19. Where did Nick and Nora stay while they were in New York?

20. What caliber gun was used to kill Julia Wolf?

BONUS—**What was the Thin Man's name?**

P. D. James

P. D. James was born in Oxford, England, and was educated at Cambridge. From 1949 to 1968, she worked for the Hospital Service, providing her with a great deal of health and medical information that she would later use in her plots. Her first novel was published in 1962; she lives in London.

1. What does P. D. stand for?

Adam Dalgliesh, intellectual yet sensitive detective of Scotland Yard, made his debut in *Cover Her Face* (1966) and has since been featured in seven of James's novels (though not always as the principal character). With each new appearance he has grown older and wiser, even more of a truly human detective.

2. From *Cover Her Face* to *Death of an Expert Witness* (1977), how far has Dalgliesh risen in rank?

3. What disease is he stricken with in the course of the novels and what is it misdiagnosed as?

4. What does the term "without portfolio" mean?

5. What is the nickname of his assistant, Detective John Massingham?

6. What is Dalgliesh doing at the opening of *A Mind to Murder* (1967)?

7. What is the setting of *A Mind to Murder*?

8. How is Enid Bolan murdered?

9. What is the name of the little coastal settlement that is the setting for *Unnatural Causes* (1967)?

10. Who is the famous mystery writer residing at the settlement?

11. What murder case begins the novel *Death of an Expert Witness*?

12. In a typical locked-room setting, how was Dr. Edwin Lorrimer killed?

13. Who discovered the body of Stella Mawson hanging from a hook in the Wren chapel?

Cordelia Gray, the twenty-two-year-old heroine of *An Unsuitable Job for a Woman* (1972), is a welcome new addition to the pantheon of great detectives, male and female alike. All signs indicate that she will be as successful a continuing character in James's novels as Adam Dalgliesh.

14. What was Cordelia's father's occupation?

15. What was unusual about her education?

16. For what detective agency is she proprietor and sole investigator?

17. Who was her first client?

18. What does Cordelia send Dagliesh during his illness?

19. What is the island setting of *The Skull Beneath the Skin* (1982)?

20. What play is to be performed there?

Peter Lovesey

Peter Lovesey was born in Whitton, Middlesex, England. He was a departmental head at Hammersmith College until 1975 when he decided to devote his full time to writing. His most famous creation is of course Sergeant Cribb, an outstanding member of the Victorian police force.

1. What is Sergeant Cribb's wife's first name?

2. What is Constable Thackeray's first name?

3. What was Thackeray's first major arrest?

4. Who is the Commissioner of the Metropolitan police force?

5. Who is Sergeant Cribb's immediate superior?

Wobble to Death **(1970), the first Sergeant Cribb mystery, places the indefatigable Scotland Yard officer trackside to solve the mystery of the death of a participant in a "wobble" at the Agricultural Hall in Islington.**

6. What is a "wobble"?

7. Who are the two favorites?

8. What were the three major prizes for the winners of the competition?

9. By what means was the frontrunner killed?

10. Who won the race and what was the total amount of distance he covered?

Another Sergeant Cribb mystery also has a sporting motif—the outlawed competition of bare-knuckles boxing.

11. What is the title of this bare-knuckled mystery?

In *Waxwork* (1978), Cribb is assigned to carry out a highly secretive inquiry into the facts concerning a newfound piece of evidence that may or may not clear a self-confessed murderess, whose date with the gallows has already been set.

12. What is the name of the convicted murderess?

13. Who is James Berry?

14. What is the newfound piece of evidence?

15. Who was the murder victim and by what means was he killed?

16. To what does the title refer?

The subject of Victorian spiritualism is explored in *A Case of Spirits* (1975) when Cribb and Thackeray are called in to investigate the apparent death by electrocution of a medium during a séance. It all started with a routine burglary investigation....

17. What was allegedly stolen?

18. What was the name of the electrocuted medium?

19. Of what exclusive group is Dr. Probert, an eminent physiologist of the University of London and one of the murder suspects, a member?

A gruesome murder brings Cribb and Thackeray to the shore during the vacation season in *Mad Hatter's Holiday* (1975).

20. What is the name of this vacation spot?

Ed McBain

Ed McBain is a pseudonym for Evan Hunter who gave up teaching in a vocational high school in New York to become a screenplay writer and novelist. Some of his screenplays include Fuzz *(1968),* The Birds *(1963), and* The Blackboard Jungle *(1955) which was based on his own novel* The Blackboard Jungle *(1954). Hunter is probably best known for his first-rate 87th Precinct series that he writes as Ed McBain, and his more recent Matthew Hope series.*

The black-haired beauty that Matthew Hope saw on the beach on Saturday paid a rather surprising visit to his law office two days later. She had been badly beaten and was terrified and in fear for her life. When her body is discovered the next day Matthew decides to find out why in *Beauty and the Beast* (1982).

1. What make of car did Michelle Harper drive?

2. Where did George Harper buy the gasoline can?

3. Mrs. Reynolds ran a boutique in the Lucy's Circle shopping complex; what was its name?

4. What did Sally Owen give each member of "the Oreo"?

5. Who was Skye Bannister?

Vicky Miller was desperate to make a comeback as a singer, but somebody out there made sure that she'd never succeed. When the killer kidnaps Vicky's daughter, Matthew Hope is more determined than ever to find out who killed his friend in *Rumpelstiltskin* (1981).

6. Name Vicky Miller's first gold record during the sixties.

7. Who was the designer of Dale O'Brien's house and the Greenery restaurant?

8. How did Gretal Heibel support herself?

9. Eddie Marshall stayed at the Marjo Motel in Caluso. Who owned the motel?

10. What did Dwayne Miller threaten to do if Vicky opened at the Greenery?

During a heatwave anything can happen, and in the 87th Precinct it does! There's an artist taking an overdose of sleeping pills and a psychopath with murder on his mind, as Detective Steve Carella works overtime trying to cool things down in *Heat* (1981).

11. Where did Anne Newman tell Detective Carella she stayed while in Los Angeles?

12. Why did the murderer turn off the air-conditioner after killing Jeremiah Newman?

13. Who was Augusta Kling's lover?

14. What kind of gun did the assailant use when he fired at Bert Kling?

15. Name the doctor who wrote the prescription for Seconal capsules for Mrs. Newman.

Detectives Carella and Kling of the 87th Precinct are looking for a murderer and a would-be murderer when television star Stan Gifford is killed during prime time, before an audience of forty million people— that's *Eighty Million Eyes* (1966).

16. Name the drug that killed comedian Stan Gifford.

17. What did the killer do to the poisoned capsule to prevent it from dissolving too quickly?

18. John Cacciatore had a nickname; what was it?

19. In what capacity did Cindy Forrest work at Vollner's Audio-Visual Components Company?

20. Paul Blaney, the assistant medical examiner, did something for the first time in his career. What was it?

John D. MacDonald

"I want story, wit, music, wryness, color, and a sense of reality in what I read and I try to get it in what I write," says John D. MacDonald and he has done just that. He started writing during World War II when he served in Intelligence in Ceylon by sending his wife short stories instead of letters. After the war he devoted himself to writing and earned a living from the short stories published in mystery magazines. He is best known for the Travis

McGee series (each title distinguished by the use of a color), "the thinking man's Robin Hood."

Travis McGee's fiancée Gretal is marked for death by the cult group she is working for when she unwittingly becomes a threat to their organization. McGee's vengeance is unmatched as he goes after the truth in *The Green Ripper* (1979).

1. Name the religious cult for which Gretal worked.

2. Gretal recognized someone as the cult leader of a church her sister-in-law had disappeared from. Who was it?

3. What name and cover story does McGee use to join the "church"?

4. The founder of the "church" is known as Sister Elena Marie. What is her real identity?

5. Funds raised by the "church" go to support what?

Travis McGee had no idea how deadly his decision was to help Cathy Kerr get her money back. Wide-eyed and innocent, she was easily conned out of the fortune her father had left her in *The Deep Blue Good-Bye* (1964).

6. What was the fortune Cathy's father brought back from India?

7. How did Allen know about the fortune?

8. McGee borrowed the *Rut Cry* to go after Allen. Who owned it?

9. Where did McGee fence the last of the stones?

10. Which one of Allen's victims did McGee nurse back to health on his boat?

In *Nightmare in Pink* (1964), Travis McGee wouldn't refuse an old friend's request to look up his sister. It seemed like the neighborly thing to do, until things got out of hand and into drugs and embezzlement and kidnapping. And it's McGee who gets snatched!

11. What was done to Charles Armister to keep him out of the way in his own corporation?

12. How did McGee end up in Toll Valley Hospital?

13. Name the three doctors doing the experiments at the hospital.

14. McGee needed a distraction in order to escape from Toll Valley Hospital. What did he do?

15. Who was the mastermind behind the takeover of Armister's corporation?

The con is on, and McGee is going to have to be a lot smarter and a great deal tougher than the vicious gang he's up against. These criminals don't just take a person's money, they take his soul as well in *Bright Orange for the Shroud* (1965).

16. What was the name of the yacht Calvin Stebber was staying on at the Cutlass Yacht Club?

17. Who was the housekeeper for Wilma and Arthur Wilkinson?

18. How much money did Wilkinson lose to the crooks?

19. To get past the cops guarding the Waxwell place what did McGee, Choak, and Arthur pose as?

20. Sam Dunning operated a charter boat out of a club in Everglades City. Name the club.

Ross Macdonald

Ross Macdonald was born near San Francisco in 1915. For over twenty years he resided in Santa Barbara and wrote mystery novels about the fascinating and changing society of his native state. He was a recipient of the Mystery Writers of America Grand Master Award and the Silver Dagger Award of the Crime Writers' Association of Great Britain.

1. What is Ross Macdonald's real name?

2. Why did he initially use a pen name?

3. Under what name did he write the first half dozen Archer stories?

4. What is Lew Archer's birthday?

The Archer volume entitled *The Name Is Archer* (1955) is actually an anthology of seven of Archer's shorter cases. In the story entitled "The Bearded Lady," his search for an old wartime buddy leads him hot on a trail of theft and murder.

5. What was his buddy's name?

6. Where did they serve together?

7. To what does the story's title refer?

In *The Zebra-Striped Hearse* (1962), Archer goes south of the border in search of a young woman. She has run off with a penniless artist whose passport bears the name of a man whose dead body has just been identified, eventually leading Archer on a trail littered with adultery, betrayal, and murder.

8. What name has the artist been passing himself under?

9. What is the name on his passport?

10. What is his real name?

11. What is the name of the young woman who he coerces into going to Mexico with him?

The Far Side of the Dollar (1965) has Archer involved with California's decadent rich. This time he is called in to investigate an alleged kidnapping of the delinquent son of a rich and powerful family.

12. From what school/institution does the boy escape?

13. What is the boy's name?

Archer's investigation eventually leads him to the seamy side of town and to an abandoned hotel where the sins of the past resurface, seeking retribution, and, once the kidnapping is solved, there is still a double murderer to be brought to justice.

14. What was the name of the hotel?

15. What is the fate of the double murderer?

16. To what does the title *The Far Side of the Dollar* refer?

In addition to his Archer novels, Macdonald has written several other mysteries featuring different investigators.

In *The Three Roads* (1948), a police lieutenant searches for his wife's lover and alleged killer.

17. What was this policeman's name?

In *Meet Me at the Morgue* (1953), a probation officer takes on the investigative role, as he tries to prove the innocence of a client.

18. What is the officer's name?

19. What is the name of the ineffectual detective he comes in contact with?

20. What do the movies *Harper* (1966) and *The Drowning Pool* (1976) have in common with the Archer novels?

BONUS—How does Macdonald sum up his relationship with his character, Archer?

Ngaio Marsh

Ngaio (pronounced Ny-o) is a Maori word for a New Zealand flower, and Ngaio Marsh is one of today's most popular mystery writers. She enjoys the same respect among her peers as does Mignon G. Eberhart and Agatha Christie. Marsh says she conjured up Inspector Alleyn during a rainy afternoon in London in 1931. She was very pleased when an early reviewer referred to Alleyn as "that nice chap," for that's just how she sees him too!

Inspector Roderick Alleyn thought it quite implausible that Pen Cuckoo could harbor any criminals, but the serene and charming vale did for the local pianist is actually murdered as she plays the opening number for the town's new show in *Overture to Death* (1939).

1. What was Idris Campanula playing on the piano when she was killed?

2. Who inadvertently gave the killer the idea for the booby trap inside the piano?

3. How did Idris trigger the booby trap which would kill her?

4. What did Miss Prentice need an onion for?

5. Why did Miss Prentice kill Idris?

Sybil Foster died very mysteriously in a rather fashionable rest home. The people involved in her life were not all they appeared to be. Inspector Alleyn is kept guessing right up to the bitter end in *Grave Mistake* (1978).

6. Who was the new beneficiary named in Sybil Foster's will?

7. Why was Claude Carter murdered?

8. What was the arrangement between Carter and Sister Jackson?

9. Who is Agatha Troy?

10. Where was the Black Alexander?

In *Death and the Dancing Footman* (1941), Jonathan Royal decided to throw a dinner party and invite people he knew were going to be antagonistic toward one another. This was Royal's idea of fun. There would be confrontations, of course, but he really didn't expect one of his guests to commit murder and another one to commit suicide.

11. Why did Mrs. Compline take her own life?

12. Who pushed Mandrake into the pond?

13. How did Nicholas manage to have the wireless set go on when he wasn't in the room?

14. Where did Inspector Alleyn find the trout fly?

15. Before Mrs. Compline killed herself, what did she do for Nicholas?

When in Rome **(1971) has Inspector Alleyn as one of a group of tourists and finding out that some of them have something to hide. This is no ordinary tour; this tour has murder as its big attraction, with some drug-dealing on the side.**

16. How did Mailer induce author Barnaby Grant to appear with the tour?

17. Major Sweet gave Alleyn something very important. What was it?

18. During the tour of the basilica how did Mailer disappear?

19. Who put Violetta's body in the sarcophagus?

20. How did Alleyn know who killed Mailer?

Ellery Queen

Frederic Dannay and Manfred B. Lee were cousins who grew up together in New York. Sharing an avid interest *in mystery stories, they decided to collaborate in writing their own stories. In 1928 they won a first prize of $7,500 for a detective novel. Between 1931 and 1971, using the pseudonym Ellery Queen, they were enormously successful writing mystery novels, most of which starred Inspector Queen and his son Ellery. They were also the co-founders of the Mystery Writers of America.*

Nino Inportuna eventually got what he wanted one way or another and that included a beautiful young wife less than half his age. But this time it cost Nino more than money. Ellery Queen is helping to sort out things in *A Fine and Private Place* (1971).

1. How was Virginia Whyte coerced into marrying Nino Inportuna?

2. To what lengths did Inportuna go to satisfy his obsession with the number nine?

3. Of all the "nine" clues which one was not a red herring?

4. What was the name of the sculpture the murderer of Nino Inportuna used?

5. Who was the mysterious "Mr. E"?

Ellery Queen met Howard Van Horn in Paris before France had become embroiled in World War II and hadn't seen him again until the day Van Horn showed up at his door in desperate need of help in *Ten Day's Wonder* (1948).

6. There was a peculiarity about all the pet names Diedrich Van Horn had for his wife Sally. What was it?

7. Who added an E to Aaron and Mattie Way's headstone, changing their surname from Way to Waye?

8. What was Mr. Van Horn buying with his large donation to the Wrightsville Art Museum Committee?

9. Where did Mr. Van Horn find the love letters Howard wrote to Sally?

10. How was Ellery going to prove that Mr. Van Horn was the blackmailer of his wife?

Getting involved in a couple's marital problems is not exactly a run-of-the-mill case for amateur sleuth Ellery Queen, but his secretary Nikki convinces him that he's the only one who can help the Lawrences before someone gets seriously hurt in *The Scarlet Letters* (1953).

11. What was distinctive about the mysterious letters Martha Lawrence received?

12. How did Martha and Van Harrison communicate to each other the whereabouts of their next rendez-vous?

13. Ellery found love letters written by Martha in Van's desk. Who did Martha really write the letters to?

14. Gossip columnist Leon Fields used another name to rent an apartment on Eighty-eighth street. What was that name?

15. What message was Harrison trying to convey to Ellery before he died?

Ellery got a different type of job this time, and it shouldn't be too difficult or so he thinks—just protect King Bendigo from assassination! And to do the job Ellery has access to unlimited resources of money and men. So how come *The King Is Dead* (1952)?

16. Why did Ellery and his father accept the responsibility of protecting King Bendigo?

17. Who was the only other person in the locked room with King Bendigo when he was shot?

18. How was the gun removed from the scene of the crime?

19. While King Bendigo always took credit for saving his brother's life, who really saved Abet from drowning?

20. Who was the head of Bendigo's PRPD?

Dorothy L. Sayers

Dorothy Leigh Sayers is recognized as one of the first women to receive a degree from Oxford. As a medieval linguist and Christian theological scholar, her knowledge and expertise are easily seen in the erudite and aristocratic Lord Peter Wimsey, who is said to have been modeled on an Oxford don of her acquaintance.

1. Where was Lord Peter Wimsey educated?

2. What is the Wimsey family motto?

3. What is Bunter's first name?

4. What were Lord Peter's and Bunter's ranks during their service in World War I?

5. Of the many things that Bunter does well, for what is Lord Peter most appreciative?

6. What was Lord Peter's wife's maiden name, and what was her profession?

In the novel *Whose Body?* (1923)...

7. Where is the first murder victim's body discovered?

8. What was unusual about it?

In *The Five Red Herrings* (1931), Lord Peter and Bunter travel to an artists' colony for a vacation. There they become involved in the investigation of the death of an artist who apparently fell from his scenic perch into a jagged ravine.

9. What was the artist's name?

10. What was the name of the artists' colony?

11. What was Lord Peter's original reason for going there?

12. What was the novel's first American title?

In *Murder Must Advertise* (1933), Lord Peter becomes a prime suspect in a murder investigation at a seemingly respectable advertising agency that has many dark secrets waiting to be revealed.

13. What is the name of the agency?

14. What is the name of the murdered copywriter?

15. What was the cause of death?

16. What was his replacement's name?

17. What is the novel's very businesslike last line?

In *The Nine Tailors* (1934), Lord Peter investigates a mysterious death in the uppermost reaches of a bell tower as the locals toll in the New Year. The mystery begins when a body is discovered in the recently opened grave of a young woman, and traces back to a

famous local robbery that had taken place many years earlier.

18. What is the name of the church noted for its famous bells?

19. For how long a period are the bells tolled for the New Year?

20. What was unusual about the recently discovered dead body?

BONUS—**What is the complete subtitle of** *The Nine Tailors?*

Dell Shannon

Dell Shannon is the author of over thirty books for which she has done thorough research on the Los Angeles Police Department, gaining firsthand knowledge of police procedures and laboratory techniques. Her novels are filled with gritty realism and strong characterizations, particularly in the Lieutenant Mendoza series.

1. What is Dell Shannon's real name?

2. What is Lieutenant Mendoza's wife's full name?

3. What are the names of their twins?

In *Streets of Death* **(1976), Mendoza and his men are up against a wave of violent crimes pervading the city streets, from muggers preying on the elderly and the**

infirm to a nonmobile invalid's disappearance. **Mendoza shifts into high gear when it turns out that one of the mugging victims is the elderly priest at the local mission church.**

4. What is his name and what is stolen from him?

5. What is unusual about the invalid's mysterious disappearance?

6. What is the name of the neighborhood eccentric who claims to have overheard a murder being planned?

In *Felony at Random* (1979), Mendoza is faced with a case of triple murder, a police sergeant shot while sitting at home, and a mysterious wave of suicides in a usually peaceful neighborhood... all while his wife is giving birth to their third child.

7. What is the name of the murdered police sergeant?

8. What precinct was he attached to?

9. What was the *modus operandi* of the triple murderer?

10. Where was young Joyce McCauley last seen before she disappeared and was reported missing?

11. What was the name of the pharmacist suspected of being a sexual degenerate and murderer?

12. What was the name of Mendoza's third child?

During the course of *The Motive on Record* (1982), Mendoza's wife entertains herself by reading factual mysteries and making plans for their upcoming vacation, while the good lieutenant confronts another series of baffling crimes.

13. What is the name of the eight-year-old murder/rape victim?

14. What school did she attend?

15. What type of reputation did the elderly murdered Mabel Otis have?

16. Where did the Mendozas go for their vacation?

17. How did the lieutenant feel about the chosen location?

The Mendozas have just returned home in *Exploit of Death* (1983) when the lieutenant is called in to investigate a suicide. Surprisingly, the Mendozas had recently met the subject on their return flight home. Or had they?

18. What was the name of the Mendozas' seatmate?

19. By what name is her body identified by her landlord and neighbors?

20. Where does the lieutenant have to go to discover her true identity?

Georges Simenon

Georges Simenon with over two hundred novels to his credit is without a doubt the most prolific international mystery author of all time. With a literary career that began at the age of sixteen, Simenon has been published in thirty-two languages. His novels are largely psychological, and by far his most famous creation is the immortal Inspector Maigret of the Paris police force.

1. What is Maigret's first name?

2. Where was he born?

3. Where is his office located?

4. What was his father's first name?

In *Maigret Goes Home* (1932), the inspector returns to his birthplace to investigate a mysterious note warning that a crime will be committed during the first Mass of the day at the local estate church. The person murdered turns out to be the elderly countess of the estate, and the cause of her death is heart failure, possibly caused by some sort of shock.

5. On what Holy day did the "murder" occur?

6. What appears to have instigated the countess's heart failure?

7. What is the name of the heir to the estate?

8. What is the name of the altar boy whom Maigret takes an interest in because he reminds him of himself when he was younger?

In *Maigret Mystified* (1932), a businessman is found dead of a gunshot wound. His body was left in his office of his pharmaceutical firm with a large amount of money missing from the company safe, thus forcing Maigret to investigate a case which might be in reality two separate ones—a murder and a robbery.

9. The man killed was M. Couchet. What was his mistress's name?

10. What was his son's name?

11. What sort of habit did his son possess?

12. How did Couchet's will divide his estate?

In *Maigret on the Defensive* (1966), the inspector is called upon to defend himself from a complaint that has been filed against him that might end his brilliant career.

13. What is the nature of this complaint?

14. Who lodged the complaint?

A strange old woman asks the inspector to help her in *Maigret and the Madwoman* (1972), only to be dismissed as a harmless old eccentric...until she is found murdered, and Maigret vows to find her killer.

15. What was the "madwoman's" name?

16. What were her last words to Maigret?

17. How was she murdered?

In *Maigret and the Loner* (1975), an anonymous telephone call provides a clue to the murder of a Parisian vagrant. The investigation leads Maigret to a popular holiday resort.

18. What is unusual about the vagrant's body?

19. What was the name of the holiday resort?

In a series of stories, Simenon invented a character nicknamed "the Little Doctor," a country doctor who uses his powers of observation (sharpened by his medical work) to solve criminal cases.

20. What is the Little Doctor's real name?

BONUS—What is the full title of the American edition of Simenon's autobiography?

Mickey Spillane

Mickey Spillane (who claims to be the most widely trans-
lated American author) forever altered the detective genre
with his own mixture of mystery, sex, and sadism. His
handling of the mystery motif reflects the dark side of
the American macho-myth of violence.

1. What is Spillane's full name?
2. What is Mike Hammer's secretary's name?
3. Who is Mike's favorite cop on the homicide squad?

Mike Hammer made his literary debut in 1947, as
Mike seeks the killer of a wartime buddy, playing the
role of judge, jury, and executioner all at once.

4. What is the title of this first Mike Hammer mystery?
5. What is the name of Mike's murdered buddy?
6. How was he killed?
7. What sentence does Hammer's one-man legal sys-
   tem mete out?
8. What is the novel's succinct last line?

In *My Gun Is Quick* (1950), a beautiful redhead is
killed by a hit-and-run, after casually chatting with

Mike the night before. Mike had nicknamed her Red, and insists to the authorities that it was murder. He sets out to find the killer because in his own words— "Wherever there's murder, there's money."

9. What was Red's real name?

10. Before she was killed, Red had mailed a letter—to whom was it addressed?

11. How was the letter signed?

12. What is the book's shocking last line?

As with the predecessors, *Vengeance Is Mine* (1950), also opens with a murder. Mike is left unconscious at the scene, and an old friend is left dead, shot with Mike's gun. The trail leads to sexy Juno Reeves, who comes on to Mike like gangbusters.

13. What was the murder victim's name?

14. What was unusual about Juno? (Remember the book's surprising last line.)

Bloody Sunrise (1965) features another Spillane cold-blooded killer/hero. This one could be billed as America's toughest espionage agent.

15. What is his name?

Me, Hood! (1969) collects two Spillane novellas ("Me, Hood!" and "Return of the Hood"), featuring a mob hitman who is hired by the cops and given an unconditional license to kill.

16. What is "the Hood's" real name?

17. What is somewhat unusual for a hitman about his educational background?

18. How does Mickey Spillane refer to his readers?

19. In what film did Spillane play Mike Hammer?

20. On what cover did Spillane's wife pose in the nude?

BONUS—What was "The Veiled Woman?"

Rex Stout

Rex Stout was born in Noblesville, Indiana. He published several nonmysteries before turning to detective fiction at the age of forty-eight. By far his most famous creation has been New York's corpulent answer to Sherlock Holmes, who with the help of his streetwise aide Archie Goodwin almost always solves the case without ever leaving his humble Manhattan abode.

1. What is Nero Wolfe's address?

2. What are the names of Wolfe's two household employees and what are their duties?

3. Who are Wolfe's three most often used surveillance operatives?

4. What is Wolfe's favorite brand of beer?

5. What is his favorite amusement?

6. What does he do for "exercise?"

7. For what affair does Wolfe leave his home once each year?

8. Who is Wolfe's equivalent of Moriarty?

9. Under what circumstances did Wolfe and Archie first meet?

10. What was Wolfe and Archie's first recorded case?

11. To what did its title refer?

12. In the book entitled *Death of a Doxy* (1966), what was the name of the doxy?

13. What other Nero Wolfe novel begins with the words "Death of..."?

14. What is the name of the group formed by several Harvard classmates in *The League of Frightened Men* (1935)?

15. With what famous person does Wolfe come in contact with in *The Doorbell Rang* (1965)?

16. What radical assertion did Rex Stout once make at a meeting of the Baker Street Irregulars?

17. In Stout's opinion what was the best detective novel that he had ever written?

18. What is unusual about this?

How did Nero Wolfe finish the following lines:

19. "To be broke is not a disgrace..."

20. "The only safe secrets are..."

BONUS—Who is the only person in New York to call Wolfe by his first name?

CLERICAL MYSTERIES

G. K. (Gilbert Keith) Chesterton

G. K. Chesterton was born in London, England, in May 1874. He had his early education at St. Paul's School in London and later he studied art at the Slade School. He was employed as a reviewer of art books for the **Bookmen** *and went on to write for other journals, including the* **Illustrated London News.** *During this time he wrote poetry, plays, novels, essays, as well as social and literary criticism. He is best remembered for his detective stories about Father Brown, the engaging priest-detective.*

1. What did George Bernard Shaw refer to as "the Chesterbelloc"?

2. Chesterton modeled his sleuthing cleric after an old friend. Who was the friend?

3. Chesterton is known as the master of what?

Chesterton wanted "to construct a comedy in which a priest should appear to know nothing and in fact

know more about crime than the criminal." To this end he created Father Brown.

The Wisdom of Father Brown (1912) is a collection of cases that were solved by the inimitable Father in his own delightful and unassuming manner.

4. In "The Absence of Mr. Glass" Father Brown enlists the aid of an eminent criminologist to help the McNat family. Name the criminologist.

5. The McNab family understood Mr. Todhunter's strange behavior when Father Brown revealed the man's true identity. Who was James Todhunter?

The complexities of a rather nasty situation do not escape Father Brown in "The Duel of Dr. Hirsch."

6. What did Father Brown discover about Dr. Hirsch and Colonel Dubosc?

7. Who offered to second for Colonel Dubosc?

8. What did the colonel say could be found in the Secretary's desk at the War Office?

William Kienzle

After his ordination in 1954, William Kienzle spent his next twenty years as a parish priest. During twelve of those years he worked as editor in chief of the **Michigan Catholic Newspaper.**

Since leaving the priesthood, Kienzle writes very successful novels of mystery and suspense that reflect his own avid interest in police work.

The first of this series of bizarre and senseless murders occurs on Ash Wednesday, and the police department of Detroit, Michigan, is stumped until Father Robert Koesler discovers that the killer is following his own code for the murders in *The Rosary Murders* (1979).

1. What did all the victims have in common?

2. What was the symbol of the rosary in each of the killings?

3. What did the murderer use as his code in choosing his victims?

4. Who was the inspector of homicide and his partner?

Detroit, Michigan is once again at the mercy of a homicidal maniac. This one leaves his victims' heads on the headless shoulders of church statues, and other sacriligious locations. Father Koesler must come to the aid of the police in tracking down this murderer in *Death Wears a Red Hat* (1980).

5. According to the coroner what did all the victims die from?

6. Ramon Toussaint's wife, Emerenciana, was a "Mombo." What was a "Mambo"?

7. Who was the "avenging angel"?

8. The last victim's head wasn't left on a statue's shoulders. Where was it left?

When the not-too-popular Monsignor Thomas Thompson disappears from a wedding reception, foul play is suspected. Father Koesler is hard put to sort out the many suspects he finds in *Mind Over Murder* (1981).

9. What prime piece of evidence was so useful to Father Koesler during his investigation?

10. Father Koesler had two newspaper friends who helped him in the case. Name them and the newspapers they worked for.

11. The Money-Man was one of the suspects. What was he guilty of?

12. What was the name of Lee Brand's boat?

Harry Kemelman

Harry Kemelman says that his initial purpose in writing is to explain the Jewish religion, using fiction as a vehicle. Before his success as a mystery writer Kemelman taught both high school and college in Boston, Massachusetts. He has had some success with a series of short stories with Professor Nicky Welt, but it is the Rabbi Small series that has won him acclaim with mystery readers.

Friday the Rabbi Slept Late (1964), the first of the very popular series with Rabbi Small and Police Chief Hugh Lanigan, has the two men working side by side to solve the murder of a local girl that had the Rabbi as a suspect!

1. The Rabbi became a murder suspect because of something the police found in his car. What was it?

2. Who was Elsbeth Bleech working for when she was killed?

3. What did Joe Serafino bribe Stella to do?

4. Name the father of Elsbeth Bleech's unborn child.

5. Where was Norman supposed to meet Elsbeth?

Ellsworth Jordon, the multimillionaire is the victim of a rather strange murder, and Rabbi Small and Chief Lanigan must once again protect their little community from a dangerous killer in *Thursday the Rabbi Walked Out* **(1978).**

6. How was Billy Green related to Ellsworth Jordon?

7. Why wasn't Lawrence Gore concerned that the unbalanced quarterly report was being delivered to Jordon?

8. Who killed Jordon and why?

9. The killer fired many shots at random in the murder room. Why?

10. What evidence did Rabbi Small have to prove the killer's identity?

THOSE INSCRUTABLE ORIENTALS

John P. Marquand

John P. Marquand considered "Mr. Moto" his literary disgrace. According to him, he wrote about the Japanese detective "to get shoes for the baby." He was very surprised when the public showed such interest in his character. Marquand went on to more serious writing and won the Pulitzer Prize in 1938 for **The Late George Apley.** *Before his death in 1960 he had written such popular novels as* **B. F's Daughter, Point of No Return,** *and* **Sincerely, Willis Wayde.**

In *No Hero* **(1935), Mr. Moto must use his wits to keep the free world from disaster.**

1. Who is the flyer that Mr. Moto gets help from in Tokyo?

2. What are Mr. Moto and Casey Lee hoping to find in Singapore before it falls into the wrong hands?

It's *Think Fast, Mr. Moto* **(1937) when he gets mixed up with a bunch of gamblers who are interested in more than rolling dice:**

3. What reason did William Hitchings have for going to Honolulu?

4. Who got the profits from the gambling?

Stopover: Tokyo (1957) is replete with the enemies of freedom planning to discredit the United States. Mr. Moto, determined to prevent this from happening, gets unexpected help from two Americans.

5. Name the two Americans.

6. What were the Americans doing in Tokyo?

Robert Van Gulik

Robert Van Gulik wrote the series of Judge Dee detective novels during the 1950s. Van Gulik, a Dutch diplomat, was also an authority on Chinese history and culture. His novels give a vivid picture of life in premodern China.

Judge Dee must take refuge in an old mountaintop monastery one very stormy night, only to find that it is the scene of some rather grisly crimes in *The Haunted Monastery* (1961).

7. What did the judge think he saw from his window in the guest house?

8. Judge Dee's Third Lady had a remedy for his headache. What was it?

9. Mr. Tsung Lee, the poet, had an ulterior motive for being in the monastery. What was it?

10. Where did Judge Dee find White Rose?

As the magistrate of Poo-Yang, Judge Dee is confronted with the cruel rape-murder of a young girl. The judge is enraged and vows that the crime will not go unavenged in *The Chinese Bell Murder* (1958).

11. Who was Sheng Pa?

12. What punishment did Judge Dee mete out to Lin Fan for his crime?

13. Ma Joong once belonged to the "brothers of the green woods." What did that mean?

Earl Derr Biggers

After graduating from Harvard University in 1907 Earl Derr Biggers began writing stories for the Saturday Evening Post. *In 1913 Biggers enjoyed his first success with* Seven Keys to Baldpate. *He is best known for his Charlie Chan detective stories, whose central character, Inspector Chan, Biggers had based on a detective he had met in Honolulu.*

In *Charlie Chan Carries On* (1930), Chan goes to the aid of his old friend Inspector Duff from Scotland Yard.

14. Who is Inspector Chan's Japanese friend and fellow detective?

15. Identify the ship that Duff has come to meet in Honolulu.

16. What was Hugh Drake strangled with?

17. Where did Ross have the safety-deposit box key hidden?

Glamorous film star Shelah Fane has been murdered and Inspector Chan is hot on the trail of the murderer when confusion strikes in the form of an unsolved crime from the past in *The Black Camel* (1929).

18. The murderer of Shelah Fane used a man's large handkerchief to wrap Miss Fane's wristwatch in order to break it. Whose handkerchief was it?

19. What was the connection between the fortune-teller Tarneverro and Denny Mayo?

20. Why didn't Shelah Fane want her emerald ring to be noticed?

The Medical Mysteries of Robin Cook

Previous to becoming a best-selling novelist, Robin Cook, pseudonym for Doctor Robert William Arthur, was an ophthalmologic surgeon. His novels dealing with the world of medicine always concern the burning issues of the

*modern medical scene. Cook strives to make his readers
better informed medical consumers, while enjoying a good
mystery.*

In *Fever* (1982), research doctor Charles Martel's daughter has leukemia, and he wants to take care of her. But his unorthodox treatment is not acceptable by law so he must use drastic measures to be near her and to defend himself against some unsavory business people from the Weinberger Cancer Institution.

1. Dr. Martel was sure he had found the reason his daughter Michelle had leukemia; what was it?

2. Who were the owners of the recycling plant that was dumping toxic waste into the river?

3. What did Martel use in the booby trap at the backdoor of his house?

4. What device did Hoyt and Ferrullo use to try to drive the Martels out of the house?

5. Who shot Dr. Martel as he left the barricaded house?

Too many surgical patients are dying at Boston Memorial Hospital. Reason enough for Dr. Kingsley's psychiatrist wife Cassie to start asking some very pertinent questions—questions that put her in a very dangerous position in *Godplayer* (1983).

6. What does S.S.D. refer to?

7. How did the victims die?

8. Where was Dr. Kingsley getting his supply of drugs?

9. Why did Cassie suspect it was her husband who tried to kill her?

10. Who was the night supervisor on ICU?

THE NEW HARD-BOILED AND TONGUE-IN-CHEEK MYSTERIES

Stuart Kaminsky

Stuart Kaminsky's Toby Peters works as a private detective in 1940s Hollywood during the Golden Age of motion pictures.

1. Before becoming a detective, what did Peters do for a living?

2. What does his brother do?

3. Who does Toby share his office with?

In **Murder on the Yellow Brick Road** (1977), during the course on his investigation into the death of a "munchkin" on the old *Wizard of Oz* set, Toby encounters a certain writer "with an ear for dialogue" who tags along with him for part of the case.

4. Who is this writer "with an ear for dialogue"?

Robert B. Parker

Robert B. Parker's Spenser, the hard-boiled ex-cop from Boston, has recently become one of the most popular of the new breed of detectives.

5. In what war did Spenser see military duty?

6. Where was his office located?

7. What was his first recorded case?

8. Who were his employers on this case?

9. For what novel did Parker receive his first Edgar Award?

10. This novel also introduced readers to Spenser's sidekick Hawk—how did they originally meet?

11. Where does most of the action in *The Judas Goat* (1978) take place?

12. What is the name of the child prostitute in *Ceremony* (1982)?

Bill Pronzini

Bill Pronzini, author of numerous novels and short stories and editor of many successful anthologies, introduced in his novel **The Snatch** *(1969) the most anonymous detective since the Continental Op.*

13. What is the name of Pronzini's detective?

14. In what city was he a practicing private detective?

Jack Lynch

Jack Lynch's Peter Bragg series features a former investigative reporter turned private detective. In the first book in the series, **Bragg's Hunch** *(1981), he is hired by a former mobster to find the source of threats that have been made against his life and his stepdaughter's.*

15. What is this former mobster's name?

16. What is the name of the desert town that used to be his headquarters?

Elmore Leonard

Elmore Leonard has been one of the most consistently good writers of the last few decades in both the western and mystery genres, yet it has only been within the last few years that he has received full recognition with such bestsellers as Stick *(1983) and* La Brava *(1984).*

17. What is Stick's real name?

18. What is his friend Rainey's real name?

19. In what previous Leonard novel did Stick make an appearance?

20. What is La Brava's full name?

Roger L. Simon

Roger L. Simon's Moses Wine made his debut in the 1973 novel The Big Fix *(later filmed with Richard Dreyfuss) and has since become recognized as a socially archetypal postsixties Philip Marlowe—a hard-boiled detective who hasn't lost the radical views of his youth.*

21. What university did Wine attend?

22. What is his aunt's name?

23. *The Big Fix* features an Abbie Hoffman-like radical named Howard Eppis—what is the name of the book he wrote?

24. What is the name of the Nevada bordello to which Wine follows the mysterious man named Jonas?

25. What is the name of the unscrupulous politician whose reelection campaign is at the heart of "the big fix"?

26. What is his opponent's name?

27. In *Peking Duck* (1979), how does one of Wine's Oriental acquaintances describe the case that Wine undertakes in China?

28. What nickname does Detective Sergeant Koontz confer on Wine?

Gregory Mcdonald

Gregory Mcdonald's Fletch series is one of the most successful tongue-in-cheek detective series of recent years. It features a laid-back journalist/beach bum who goes by the name of Fletch.

29. What is Fletch's full name?

30. For what paper is he a reporter?

31. What proposition does a mysterious millionaire offer Fletch at the opening of *Fletch* (1974)?

32. In *Fletch and the Man Who* (1983), who is the man who?

Mcdonald also created Flynn, a CIA counterpart for Fletch, in another series of mysteries, such as *The Buck Passes Flynn* (1983) where the entire world economy is placed in jeopardy.

33. What is Flynn's full name?

34. When he is not working as a governmental operative, what does he do for a living?

35. In *The Buck Passes Flynn,* where are the three locations initially affected by an induced currency glut?

36. On whom does Flynn stage a "successful" assassination attempt?

Daniel Odier

Daniel Odier first came to full recognition in the United States when one of his caper novels, Diva *(1982), was made into a critically acclaimed New Wave film. The novel introduced his Nick and Nora of the New Wave set, Gorodish and Alba, involving them in a mystery caused by the mix-up of two very important tapes.*

37. What did each tape contain?

38. What is the diva's real name?

39. How old were Gorodish and Alba when they first entered into their highly unconventional partnership?

40. Under what pen name does Odier write his Gorodish and Alba novels?

Mini-mysteries: The Short Story

1. What is considered by many to have been the most successful and popular mystery short story of the Victorian era?

2. What is the name of the short story that introduced the character of reformed safecracker Jimmy Valentine?

Clifford Halifax, M.D., appeared in several short stories of the Edwardian period as a medical detective character and as a pseudonymous collaborator of Mrs. L. T. Meade on many of her short stories.

3. Who was Halifax the pseudonym for?

Another famous character/pen name was the dashing detective Dick Donovan.

4. Who was Donovan the pseudonym for?

"The Vanishing Diamonds" by M. McDonnel Bodkin features, in addition to the missing diamonds of the title, an imposter for a detective, and a box with a secret compartment.

5. At whose wedding were the diamonds stolen?

6. What is the name of the story's real detective?

Edwardian author William Hope Hodgson wrote a series of stories featuring the first parapsychologist detective of English literature.

7. What was this psychic detective's name?

8. What was his address?

9. To whom does he relate his many adventures?

10. What is the usual setting for his tale-telling?

11. What was the *Jarvee*?

Jacques Futrelle authored a series of stories featuring a character nicknamed "the Thinking Machine." His most famous case was "The Problem of Cell 13," which involved him escaping from a maximum-security facility in order to prove that a rational man could literally think himself out of any situation.

12. What was "the Thinking Machine's" real name?

13. With whom does he make a bet that he can indeed escape from a maximum-security prison?

14. What was the name of the prison?

15. What were the three things that "the Thinking Machine" requested when he was incarcerated?

Harry Kemelman, in addition to creating the Rabbi David Small novels, also wrote a series of short stories

featuring a New England academic cast in the mode
of a contemporary "thinking machine."

16. What was this scholar's name?

17. What subject did he teach?

18. What was the ambulatory title of the collection of
    short stories featuring this scholar?

19. Who was the narrator of these stories?

20. What famous literary/historical pair were featured
    in a series of mystery short stories by Lillian de la
    Torre?

BONUS—**What was Lillian de la Torre's real name?**

Whodunit?

*The "whodunit" has always been a favorite of mystery
fans. A crime that is inexplicable, that mystifies and
perplexes, that's what arouses the readers' curiosity like
nothing else can. And no respectable whodunit would be
complete without a red herring or two.*

1. What is a red herring?

2. Where did the term "red herring" originate?

**One of the most baffling real life whodunits is a crime
that was committed in Pukekawa, New Zealand, in
1970. David Yallop has recounted the story of the**

double murder óf a husband and wife in a book and a
screenplay (1983) both titled *Beyond Reasonable Doubt*.

3. Name the people who were murdered.

4. Who was the first one to arrive at the farmhouse?

5. What did the first person at the farmhouse find?

6. When Mr. Dembar realized something was wrong
   at the farmhouse whom did he call before he called
   the police?

7. Who was the inspector in charge of the case?

8. The police arrested an ex-boyfriend of the dead
   woman. Name him.

9. What did the police do to insure conviction of the
   man they had arrested?

10. The man convicted of the murder was released
    nine years later through the efforts of the prime
    minister. Identify the prime minister.

Based on Fact

**All of the following fictional works were based on, or
connected with, real people and/or events. Identify
the source for each.**

1. *Compulsion* (novel by Meyer Levin; film directed by
   Richard Fleischer)

2. *Badlands* (film directed by Terrence Malick)

3. *The Executioner's Song* (novel by Norman Mailer; TV-movie directed by Lawrence Shiller).

4. *The Book of Daniel* (novel by E. L. Doctorow; film directed by Sidney Lumet)

5. *Rope* (film directed by Alfred Hitchcock)

6. *Winterset* (play by Maxwell Anderson; film directed by Alfred Santell)

7. *Psycho* (novel by Robert Bloch; film directed by Alfred Hitchcock)

8. *The Daughter of Time* (novel by Josephine Tey)

9. *In Cold Blood* (novel by Truman Capote; film directed by Richard Brooks)

10. *Death Scream* (TV movie directed by Richard T. Heffron)

Surprise Mystery Authors

Many famous writers have turned their pens to the mystery genre after having established themselves in some other area. In some cases they have incorporated aspects of the detective story into their other works, or they have used the genre as a vehicle for literary exercise. And of course, there are others who wrote them just for the fun of it.

William Faulkner's saga of Yoknapatawpha County includes a volume entitled *Knight's Gambit* (1949) in

which one of the characters takes on the role of detective in a series of mystery stories.

1. What is this character's name?

2. What is his profession?

Edgar Box is the pseudonym used by a well-known author for his series of mysteries featuring Peter Cutler Sargeant III, a Harvard graduate.

3. What is Sargeant's occupation?

4. Who is Edgar Box?

A. A. Milne, the author of the Winnie the Pooh stories, also wrote a whodunit entitled *The Red House Mystery* (1922), featuring an amateur detective who was sometimes nicknamed "Madman."

5. What is "Madman's" real name?

Antonia Fraser, the acclaimed historian and biographer of Mary, Queen of Scots, is also the author of a series of mysteries featuring a dynamic female TV-interviewer with a propensity for investigative reporting.

6. What is this interviewer's name?

7. What is the name of the convent school she had attended in her youth, and returns to to sort out a mystery in the novel *Quiet as a Nun* (1977)?

The prolific science/science fiction author Isaac Asimov has written on almost every subject imaginable and is no stranger to the mystery genre. Two of his science-fiction novels (*The Caves of Steel* and *The Naked Sun*) use elements of the mystery within a traditional SF plot. He has also excelled in the more conventional mystery genre as is evidenced in the collections of his short stories featuring a group called the Black Widowers.

8. What is the name of the Black Widowers' waiter who in the debut story masters "The Acquisitive Chuckle?"

Asimov also wrote the mystery novel *Murder at the ABA* (1976), where fictional author Darius Just investigates the death of a fellow author at the convention for the American Booksellers Association.

9. At what hotel was the convention held?

10. What covinces Darius that author Giles Devore's death was murder?

Louis L'Amour, America's current best-selling author of westerns, wrote several detective stories for magazines during his early years as a writer. They were recently collected in an anthology entitled *The Hills of Homicide* (1983). Three of the stories ("Dead Man's Trail," "With Death in His Corner," and "The Street of the Lost Corpses") feature a recurring detective character named Kip Morgan.

11. Before becoming "a private operator," what did Kip do for a living?

12. What did this character have in common with L'Amour?

Prior to writing the mammoth bestseller *The Far Pavilions*, M. M. Kaye wrote several mysteries set in exotic locales. The first one was recently rereleased under a new title, *Death in Zanzibar*.

13. What was its title in the original 1959 edition?

Though Ray Bradbury is primarily known for his work in science fiction and fantasy, he has also authored many mystery stories for such 1940s magazines as *Detective Tales* and *Dime Mystery Magazine*. Just recently he has finished his first full-length mystery novel.

14. What is the title of this latest addition to Bradbury's long list of credits?

Joyce Carol Oates, one of the most prolific writers of the current literary scene, having mastered the Gothic mode with *Bellefleur,* and the nineteenth century romance with *A Bloodsmoor Romance,* turned her talents to the mystery genre with *The Mysteries of Winterhurn* (1983).

15. What is the name of her detective character?

16. What is the name of his last case?

Gifted musician, composer, talk-show host, and performer Steve Allen has written books on a variety of subjects. *The Talk Show Murders* (1982) concerns a murderer who preys on talk-show guests, killing them while the program is on the air.

17. On whose talk show does the first murder occur?

18. What is the name of the private investigator who lends Steve Allen a hand and ends up solving the case on nationwide television?

Umberto Eco, critically acclaimed specialist in semiotics and esthetics, had an international bestseller with his first novel, *The Name of the Rose* (1983), which could be simplistically described as a medieval murder mystery set in a monastic abbey.

19. What is the name of Eco's monk-turned-detective?

20. What was the monk's order?

Whodunit II?

Who killed...

1. Elsbeth Bleech?

2. Mr. Spenalzo?

3. Bernie Pryde?

4. E. D. Kimball?

5. Miriam Cromer?

6. Miles Archer?

7. Stephen Norton?

8. James Butler Hickok?

9. Penn Wentworth?

10. Enoch J. Drebber?

NEW TALENT

Liza Cody

Liza Cody who resides in Somerset, England, won the John Creasey Award for a best first mystery novel in England and was nominated for the Mystery Writers of America's Edgar Award for the best mystery novel published in the United States in 1981.

Deirdre Jackson is dead in an auto accident. Her parents aren't satisfied that it was an accident, and Anna Lee has agreed to find out all she can about the events surrounding Deirdre's death in *Dupe* (1981).

1. Alastair Driver told Anna that he smelled something peculiar near the accident. What was it?

2. During her investigation what major crime did Anna uncover?

3. Where was Deirdre really murdered?

Anna Lee finds herself at the mercy of some vicious kidnappers when she goes to the aid of young Verity Hewit, and how the two of them must work on an escape plan before they are murdered in *Bad Company* (1982).

4. Why was Verity kidnapped?

5. Who gave Bernie Schiller the information leading to the kidnappers identities?

6. Anna gave nicknames to three of the kidnappers. What were they?

7. What is the name of the agency Anna Lee works for?

Karin Berne

Sue Bernell and Michaela Karni have already had some success in writing magazine articles and television scripts. Now, writing together under the pseudonym Karin Berne they have proven to be first-rate authors with their novel of mystery and romance, **Bare Acquaintances** *(1985).*

8. Ellie received a bribe from Lou Smith for information about Mannie Blanco. What form did the bribe take?

9. How did Ellie prevent the murderer from shooting Mark Devlin?

10. What did Dennis Devlin wrongly assume that Ellie was going to do with the tape?

Nathan Aldyne

Nathan Aldyne is one of the new breed of mystery authors writing out of Boston. His unlikeliest of detective duos—real-estate agent Clarisse Lovelace and gay bartender Daniel Valentine—are destined to become the gay community's Nick and Nora of the eighties.

In *Vermilion* (1980), they attempt to get to the bottom of the brutal murder of a young hustler of Boston's Combat Zone.

11. What is the name of the bar that Valentine works at?

12. What was the name of the murdered hustler?

13. What is the name of the hard-nosed police lieutenant who is hellbent on pinning the murder on someone within the gay community?

14. To what does the title *Vermilion* refer?

15. What is the setting of *Cobalt* (1982), the second Valentine-Lovelace mystery?

Bill Adler and Thomas Chastain

Though neither these two gentlemen are strangers to the mystery field, they scored their biggest bestseller with their 1983 solve-it-yourself mystery, **Who Killed the Robins Family?**—*awarding a grand prize of $10.000 to the person with the best solution.*

16. What is the book's full title?

17. How many Robins are there?

18. What are their first names?

19. Which member of the family has a different last name?

20. What is the name of their family butler?

Radio

Radio had its heyday from the thirties to the fifties with mystery and suspense shows enjoying immense popularity, before so many of its stars and listeners had made the transition to television.

1. "I Love a Mystery" (NBC 1939) was a fast-paced adventure serial about three young men and their detective agency. Name the writer of the serial.

2. What was the motto of the A-1 Detective Agency?

3. Who played Doc Long on the show?

4. As "The Fat Man" (ABC 1946) opens, Brad Runyon (played by J. Scott Smart) steps on the scale in a drugstore. How much does he weigh?

5. Name the actor who played Lieutenant MacKenzie.

6. "The Shadow" was first heard on CBS in 1930 but was not a huge success until Orson Welles took over the role in 1937. Who played Margo Lane on the show?

7. What did The Shadow learn in the Orient?

8. In his closing words on each show what does the Shadow say "bears bitter fruit"?

9. Alan Ladd starred in a series on ABC in 1948 as Dan Holiday, mystery writer. What was Holiday's profession before turning to mystery writing?

10. Dan Holiday ran an ad in a newspaper which read "Adventure wanted, will go anywhere—will do anything." Identify the newspaper it appeared in.

11. In 1949 over CBS radio Charles Russell debuted as a freelance insurance investigator on "Yours Truly, Johnny Dollar." Name the actor who starred as Johnny Dollar during 1950 to 1952.

12. Johnny Dollar professed to be a confirmed bachelor as long as he pursued what?

13. "Sorry, Wrong Number" was one of the most popular stories done on "Suspense Theatre" which debuted on CBS in 1942 and ran for twenty years. Identify the sound-effects artist on "Sorry, Wrong Number."

14. "Sorry, Wrong Number" was adapted for radio from a story by what author?

15. Name the actress who played the part of Mrs. Stevenson with such intensity that she collapsed at the conclusion of the show.

16. When "Nick Carter, Master Detective" debuted on Mutual in 1943 the title role was played by an opera singer turned radio actor. Name him.

17. Identify Nick's secretary and name the actress who played the role.

18. One of fiction's most popular detectives, Sam Spade, debuted in his own series on CBS in 1946 starring Howard Duff. Name the actress who played his secretary Effie Perrine.

19. What was the first thing that Sam usually asked his prospective clients?

20. In what city did Sam have his office?

21. A book publisher and his wife mixed up in one crime after another was the premise for "Mr. and Mrs. North" on CBS in 1942. Who were the last actor and actress to play the Norths on radio?

22. The Norths had a cab driver friend who was very talkative. Identify him and the actor who played him.

23. Michael Shayne was first heard on the West Coast Don Lee Network in 1944. Name the actor who played Shayne.

24. Who wrote the novels from which the show was adapted?

25. "Murder and Mr. Malone," based on the Craig Rice novels, debuted on ABC in 1947. How was Malone introduced on the show?

26. Name the actor who played John J. Malone.

27. The most popular fictional detective of all, Sherlock Holmes, made his debut on NBC in 1930. Name the actors who first played Holmes and his friend Dr. Watson.

28. On the early shows Dr. Watson invited the interviewer to his study and offered him something. What did Watson offer?

29. The last shows were produced by the BBC in London during 1955. Who played Holmes's archenemy Professor Moriarty?

30. From what Gilbert and Sullivan operetta was the Sherlock Holme's theme music adapted?

ON THE STAGE

John Pielmeier

Educated at Catholic University of America, John Pielmeier started writing plays in 1970. He did some acting at the New York Shakespeare Festival but found writing more to his liking. He has received Shubert and National Endowment Fellowships and is a member of the New Dramatists.

In "Agnes of God" (1982) psychiatrist Dr. Martha Livingstone's new patient is a very disturbed nun trying to live with a secret too terrible for her to accept.

1. Name the actress who played Dr. Livingstone in the original Broadway production of the play.

2. Why did Sister Agnes stop eating?

3. Who played Sister Agnes?

4. It appears that Sister Agnes enjoys doing one particular thing. What is it?

Ira Levin

Ira Levin won the Mystery Writers of America award for the best first novel of the year in 1953 for A Kiss Before Dying. *Levin is multitalented and is a well-known novelist and playwright. Many of his books and plays have also been produced on the screen.*

Levin's play "Deathtrap" (1978) centers on playwright Sidney Bruhl who hasn't had a hit play the last four times out. In desperation Bruhl decides to steal a former student's work and present it as his own.

5. Who were the actor and actress who play Sidney and Myra Bruhl in the play's original Broadway production?

6. What is Myra doing while Sidney and Clifford discuss the manuscript?

7. After wiping the garrotte clean what does Sidney wrap the body in?

Robert Marasco

"Child's Play" (1969) produced by David Merrick on Broadway received five Tony awards. Author Robert Marasco, a Fordham University graduate was cited that year in a Variety poll for the New York Drama Critics as the most promising playwright.

St. Charles School for boys seems to be turning into a sinister field of battle as one boy after another is physically abused by the other boys in "Child's Play" (1969).

8. What were the boys playing in the gym just before they attacked Freddy Banks (Robbie Reed)?

9. One of the teachers was obsessed with the idea that the school was his domain. Identify the teacher and the actor who played that role on the stage.

10. Why was the boy, McArdle (Lloyd Kramer), being suspended?

Anthony Shaffer

Anthony Shaffer was educated at Cambridge University after which he became a barrister but soon left the law for a career in writing. With his first play, "Sleuth" (1970) Shaffer became internationally known as a playwright.

The two main characters, Andrew Wyke (Anthony Quayle) and Milo Tindle (Keith Baxter), in "Sleuth" put their heads together to determine the future of Wykes' wife Marguerite who is Tindle's lover.

11. Andrew gave Marguerite something that he never liked on their honeymoon. What was it?

12. Andrew Wyke writes detective stories. Name the detective hero of his books.

13. Where did Milo hide Tea's stocking?

W. Somerset Maugham

Born in Paris in 1874 and raised in England, W. Somerset Maugham knew as a young child that he wanted to be a writer. By 1908 he had definitely arrived in the literary world with four of his works playing simultaneously in London theaters. Maugham's genius lay in being able to revive the oldest of themes, relacquer it, and make it look as good as new.

"The Letter" (1927) a short story from Maugham's 1926 collection *The Casuarina Tree* was one of his personal favorites. He adapted the tale of infidelity and murder to the stage where it was a huge success in London and America.

14. After the murder in whose possession is the letter?

15. In the Broadway production who starred as Leslie Crosbie?

16. When Leslie was released from prison where did her husband suggest they move to?

17. To pass the time in prison what did Leslie do?

Agatha Christie

Agatha Christie, the grande dame of mystery and suspense, won the New York Drama Critics' Circle Award in 1954–1955 for the year's best foreign play with "Witness for the Prosecution." She based the play on her short story of the same title.

18. Who starred as the accused Leonard Vole in the play?

19. Who was to inherit Miss French's fortune before she changed her will naming Leonard Vole the beneficiary?

20. How many women were serving on the jury?

At the Movies

In *Rear Window* (1954) James Stewart portrays a free-lance photographer L. B. Jeffries who is laid up with a broken leg.

1. To relieve his boredom what does Jeffries do?

2. Jeffries sees a neighbor across the courtyard commit a murder. Who portrayed the neighbor?

3. What was the neighbor's name in the film?

4. In what way was Stella indispensable to Jeff in the film?

Barbara Stanwyck played an invalid, Leona Stevenson, who overhears her own murder being plotted in the 1948 suspense thriller *Sorry, Wrong Number.*

5. Who co-starred as her husband?

6. Why did Leona's husband Henry want her dead?

7. What pertinent fact regarding her health did Henry keep from Leona?

8. What part did actor Wendell Corey play in the film?

Victor Grandison is a writer and radio announcer of rather grisly mystery stories in *The Unsuspected* (1947).

9. Althea and Oliver Keane discover that Victor has been embezzling from Matilda's inheritance. Who portrayed the Keanes in the film?

10. On the pretext of being Matilda's husband, Steve Horward gains entrance to the house. Why is he really there?

11. What part did Joan Caulfield play in the film?

12. Why did Victor's car crash with Oliver in it?

In *Wait Until Dark* (1967), Sam Hendrix unwittingly smuggles heroin into New York where three desperate criminals are waiting to take it from him.

13. Who played the double-crossing model Lisa?

14. How does Carlino gain entrance to the Hendrix apartment?

15. Where is the heroin hidden?

16. Who played the criminal Mike Talman?

The "Bulldog Drummond" series of movies featured an ex-British army officer in search of adventure.

17. Who played Drummond in the 1929 film *Bulldog Dummond*?

18. Who played his trusted sidekick Algy in the same film?

19. Who played Scotland Yard Inspector Nielson in the 1930s series of films?

20. What was the title of the 1951 film that featured Walter Pidgeon as Drummond?

Becoming obsessed with the portrait of a woman that he sees in a store window leads Professor Richard Wanley to murder and blackmail in *The Woman in the Window* (1944).

21. What is the name of the actress who portrayed the woman in the painting?

22. Why did the professor try to do away with Heidt?

23. Richard Wanley was a professor of what?

24. What was the unexpected ending to this film?

Jack, played by John Travolta, rescues a girl from an automobile crash and becomes involved in murder in *Blow Out* (1981).

25. What part does actor Peter Boyden play in the film?

26. Jack just happened to be at the scene of the accident. Why?

27. In the film, who portrayed Burke, the man who shot out the tire?

28. Name the movie in which Jack uses his recording of Sally's death scream.

In *Psycho* (1960) the suspense is killing. Norman Bates operates a very unusual kind of motel.

29. How did Norman's mother die in the film?

30. Who portrayed Sheriff Chambers and his wife?

31. What part did John Gavin play in the film?

32. In the shower scene, what was used to simulate blood?

***Laura* (1944) is a classic mystery tale with Gene Tierney as the lovely Laura whose murder Lieutenant McPherson (Dana Andrews) is positively fascinated by.**

33. In the film what is the name of the artist who paints Laura's portrait?

34. Lieutenant McPherson said it calmed his nerves to play with a small puzzle he carried in his pocket. What kind of puzzle was it?

35. Who played Bessie the maid?

36. Where did Lyedecker hide the rifle?

Finding *The Maltese Falcon* (1941) keeps Sam Spade (Humphrey Bogart), private eye, knee deep in murder and mayhem.

37. The actor who portrayed Captain Jacoby was relat-

ed to the director of the film. Name the actor, the director, and how they were related.

38. What scent did Joel Cairo (Peter Lorre) use on his business cards?

39. Who played the neurotic gunsel Wilmer?

40. In the first film version of *The Maltese Falcon* (1931), who portrayed Sam Spade?

Beginning with the first film in 1934, "The Thin Man" series of the detective adventures of Nick and Nora Charles was and still is highly successful and popular.

41. In *The Thin Man Goes Home* (1944), Nick's parents are introduced to movie audiences. Name the actor and actress who portrayed the parents.

42. In which one of "The Thin Man" films did James Stewart play a suspect?

43. Which film in the series introduced the baby Nick Charles, Jr.?

44. "The Thin Man" series was taken from a novel by what famous mystery writer?

In *The Detective* (1954), G. K. Chesterton's delightful and priestly sleuth, Father Brown, is out to recover some stolen art treasure.

45. Father Brown is deftly played by whom?

46. What art treasure was stolen?

An insurance salesman and the beautiful woman who coerces him into murder are basic ingredients for a first-rate thriller in *Double Indemnity* (1944).

47. What two famous mystery writers did the script for the film?

48. Who narrates the story in the film?

49. What was Barbara Stanwyck's name in the film?

50. Who portrayed the claims investigator, Mr. Keyes?

Ellery Queen—Master Detective **(1940) was the first of a new series of Queen movies.**

51. The same actor portrayed Ellery in the first four films during 1940 and 1941. Name him.

52. Who played Ellery's girl Friday Nikki in those films?

53. Who was the character actor who portrayed Ellery's father, Inspector Richard Queen?

In 1978 Robin Cook's best-selling medical mystery novel *Coma* was made into a movie of the same name.

54. The director of the film also has a medical degree. Name him.

55. Who portrayed Dr. Susan Wheeler in the film?

56. Where are the comatose patients bodies transferred?

57. What famous television detective played a bit part as one of the victims in the film?

58. What is the Jefferson Institute?

In the psychological murder mystery, *Dressed to Kill* (1980), a homicidal maniac is on the loose.

59. Name the actor and actress who portrayed Mr. and Mrs. Mike Miller.

60. Where were the museum sequences actually filmed?

61. What part did actor Keith Gordon play in the film?

62. Who portrayed the psychiatrist Dr. Elliott in the film?

The Fan (1981) is the film adaptation of playwright Bob Randall's first novel, *The Fan* (1977). It deals with the obsession of a fan, Douglas Breen, for Broadway star Sally Ross.

63. What is the name of the apartment building that Sally Ross lives in?

64. Name the actor who portrays Douglas Breen.

65. Breen attacks Sally's secretary, played by Maureen Stapleton and slashes her face. What is the secretary's name?

66. What is the next thing Breen does with the bloody knife after slashing the maid Elsa's throat?

67. Name the new show in which Sally is supposed to star.

In *Anatomy of a Murder* (1959), lawyer Paul Biegler (James Stewart) is hired to defend a confessed murderer. It's a sensational trial that really stirs up Biegler's quiet little town.

68. Who was Pie Eye in the film?

69. What is Lieutenant Manion on trial for?

70. A famous television comedienne and her husband had featured roles in the film. Name the comedienne and her husband.

71. What line did Lieutenant Manion's defense take?

72. The dead man's daughter, Mary Pliant, had evidence of her father's crime. What was that evidence?

73. The prosecuting attorney in the Army-McCarthy hearings, Joseph Welsh, appeared in a featured role in the film. What was the role he played?

Two sweet but eccentric old maids living in the old family mansion and caring for their nephew Teddy, who believes he's President Theodore Roosevelt, always have an empty room for rent in *Arsenic and Old Lace* (1944).

74. Whenever an elderly gentleman inquires about the room for rent what refreshments do Abby and Martha serve their guest?

75. What does Mortimor, Teddy's brother, find in the window seat?

76. Older brother Jonathan Brewster arrives at the house with his personal plastic surgeon Dr. Einstein. Who portrays Dr. Einstein in the film?

77. Nephew Teddy disposes of the bodies for his aunts by burying them in the cellar. What does Teddy think they all died from?

78. Who played Mr. Witherspoon, the head of Happy Dale Sanitarium?

Lovers Frank Chambers and Cora Papadakis are certain that their road to happiness depends on getting rid of Cora's husband Nick in *The Postman Always Rings Twice* (1981).

79. Cora is just about to murder Nick while he takes a bath and is interrupted in her attempt. What was the interruption?

80. How does Nick finally die?

81. What does lawyer Katz accept as his fee for getting Frank and Cora acquitted?

82. Name the actor who portrayed Nick in the film.

Broken-down private eye Ira Wells (Art Carney) and Hollywood kook Margo Sperling (Lily Tomlin) are thrown together when she asks him to find her cat in *The Late Show* (1977).

83. Who potrayed informant bartender Charlie Hatter in the film?

84. Margo's cat was stolen by whom?

85. Name the actor who plays Wells's partner Harry Regan.

In *The Dark Mirror* (1946) Olivia DeHaviland plays the dual role of twins Terry and Ruth Collins, although identical in appearance, one of them is a murderess.

86. Police Lieutenant Stevenson enlists the aid of psychologist Dr. Scott Elliott, in trying to discover which twin committed the murder. Who played the doctor?

87. Terry and Ruth Collins alternated at a job in the medical building where no one knew they were twins. What job was it?

88. How did Ruth get Terry to confess to the murder?

89. Who portrayed Lieutenant Stevenson in the film?

Dr. Ben McKenna (James Stewart) becomes *The Man Who Knew Too Much* (1956) while traveling by bus across French Morocco with his family on a vacation that is far from the leisurely one he expected.

90. In a Marrakesh marketplace a man made up to look like an Arab is stabbed. Identify the character in the film and the actor who portrayed him.

91. What did the dying man tell Dr. McKenna?

92. A song from the film won the Academy Award. Name the song.

93. Doris Day portrays Dr. McKenna's wife in the film. What is her name?

94. Name the actor who was featured in the film as the assassin.

In *The Big Steal* (1949), Robert Mitchum is hired to recover a stolen payroll.

95. What was his name in the movie?

96. How much was the payroll worth?

97. Who played Captain Blake?

98. Where did the thieves flee with the payroll?

In *Shadow of a Doubt* (1943) Joseph Cotten portrays Charlie Oakley—a man returning to his hometown after a long absence, hoping to conceal his murderous past.

99. Hume Cronyn, as Herbie Hawkins, has a hobby in the film. What is his hobby?

100. Who portrayed Detective Jack Graham in the film?

101. Oakley's niece Charlie Newton (Teresa Wright) has proof that he is "the Merry Widow" murderer. What is the proof?

102. How does Oakley try to do away with his niece?

Chinatown (1974) is a bizarre murder mystery with Jack Nicholson as private eye J. J. Gittas and Faye Dunaway as the *femme fatale* Evelyn Mulray.

103. The director appears in the film as an unnamed gangster who knifes Gittas. Name him.

104. Whose autographed portrait hangs on the wall in Gittas's office?

105. Evelyn Mulwray has an incestuous relationship with her father in the film. Identify Evelyn's father and name the actor who portrayed him.

106. Who plays Lieutenant Escobar in the film?

Sean Boyd (James Brolin), a truck driver, is the distraught father of a daughter who has been kidnapped in *The Night of the Juggler* (1980).

107. Before he became a truck driver what was Boyd's occupation?

108. Cliff Gorman portrays the disturbed kidnapper in the film. What is his name?

109. In creating the chase scenes in the film, how many cars were actually demolished?

110. Who portrayed Lieutenant Tonelli in the film?

James Stewart appears in *Vertigo* (1958) as ex-police detective Scottie Ferguson whose friend, Gavin Elster, asks him to investigate his wife's bizarre behavior.

111. Name the actress who plays both Madelaine and Judy in the film.

112. Madelaine believes she is a reincarnation of whom?

113. Having vertigo, Scottie is helpless as Madelaine leaps to her death from the bell tower of an old mission. Name the mission.

114. Which of the actors in the film suffers from vertigo in real life?

115. What convinces Scottie that his case has been a hoax from the very beginning?

Humphrey Bogart stars as Raymond Chandler's hard-boiled private eye Philip Marlowe in an exciting film adaptation of Chandler's novel *The Big Sleep* (1946).

116. Marlowe facetiously introduces himself to Carmen (Martha Vickers) as whom?

117. Name the actress who is featured as the clerk in the Acme Bookshop.

118. What is the make of the car the police fished out of the water at Lido Pier?

119. Who does Louis Jean Heidt portray in the film?

120. Identify actress Lauren Bacall in the film.

ON TELEVISION

The mystery has always been well represented on all major and syndicated television networks. Detectives have come and gone in all shapes, sizes, and infirmities with shows done factually, humorously, and in more recent years, romantically. From "Charlie Chan" to "Remington Steele," the mystery program is here to stay.

1. In "The Amazing Chan and the Chan Clan," an animated cartoon series, what was notable about the actor who provided the voice of Charlie Chan?

2. Though "Arrest and Trial" only lasted one full season (September 1963–1964), its format was truly noteworthy—what was it? (The series featured Ben Gazzara, Chuck Conners, and John Larch.)

3. What was the title of the episode of "The Avengers" that featured Mrs. Peel's (Diana Rigg) departure and the introduction of Tara King (Linda Thorson)? (The show dealt with an amnesia-inducing drug.)

4. Who played Steed's wheelchair-bound superior known as "Mother"?

5. Who were Baretta's two commanding officers?

6. Where did Baretta live?

7. Out of what precinct did he work?

8. Why did Barnaby Jones come out of retirement?

9. What was the name of the law firm to which Burl Ives, Joseph Campanella, and James Farentino belonged to in the "lawyers" segments of "The Bold Ones?"

10. Who played Boston Blackie on the short-lived TV-series of the same name?

11. Gene Barry played debonair millionaire LAPD chief Amos Burke in the TV-series "Burke's Law." During its last season the title was changed, as was his occupation. What was the new series' name?

12. In the 1958 *Charlie Chan* TV-series who played Charlie Chan . . . his Number One Son?

13. What was his Number One Son's first name?

14. On "Checkmate" who played Checkmate Inc.'s mentor/theoretician/criminologist, and what was his name on the series?

15. The anthology series "Climax" once featured a TV adaptation of Raymond Chandler's *The Long Goodbye*—who played Philip Marlowe?

16. What was the name of the TV-series that introduced American audiences to Patrick McGoohan as NATO agent John Drake?

17. What was the title of the miniseries/pilot for the series *Eischied*?

18. What was the name of Earl Eischied's pet cat?

19. Who murdered Dr. Richard Kimble's wife on the TV-series *The Fugitive*?

20. What was his name and who played him?

21. What were the four titles of the NBC series involving Kate Mulgrew as the wife of Lieutenant Columbo?

22. For what paper was she a part-time reporter?

23. What was her daughter's name?

24. Who was the successful attorney who agreed to hire Martin Kazinski, a novice lawyer who earned his degree while serving a prison term on the TV-series "Kaz?"

25. What was the name of the short-lived TV-series that featured Khigh Dhiegh (who had played the evil archenemy Wo-Fat on "Hawaii Five-O") as an oriental detective?

26. What was the name of the pilot for the TV-series "Kojak?"

27. Who was Demosthenes?

28. What was the name of the first crime show to be set during the Roaring Twenties?

29. What was the alternate title for "The Lone Wolf" TV-series featuring Louis Hayward as Mike Lanyard?

30. For what firm did Michael Longstreet work on "Longstreet"?

31. How did he go blind?

32. What was the name of his seeing-eye dog?

33. In the TV-series "Man Against Crime," what was unusual about New York private eye Mike Barnett (played by Ralph Bellamy)?

34. Who played his brother on the summer replacement series?

35. Who played Mike Shayne on the TV-series of the same name?

36. What was Mr. North's profession on "Mr. and Mrs. North?"

37. Who composed the theme for the "Peter Gunn" series?

38. What was Gunn's address?

39. Who played the jazz-club owner who was affectionately known as "Mother"?

40. What was the name of "the Outsider," an ex-con private eye played by Darren McGavin on "The Outsider?"

41. Who starred in "The Protectors"?

42. Who played the county coroner on the TV-series "Quincy"?

43. What was Quincy's favorite restaurant hangout?

44. On "Richard Diamond, Private Detective," who played Diamond's (David Janssen's) answering service named "Sam"?

45. What was Sam's most distinguishing characteristic?

46. What was the name of Diamond's girl friend and who played her?

47. What was the title of the show when it was placed into syndication?

48. Who created the TV-series "Richie Brockelman, Private Eye?"

49. What was its theme song?

50. Who was Richie's first client?

51. With what other TV detective did Richie once collaborate?

52. What was next door to 77 Sunset Strip?

53. Who worked there?

54. What ninety-minute detective show was shown on a rotating basis with "The CBS Tuesday Night Movie" and "Hawkins" starring Jimmy Stewart?

55. What was the name of the TV-series that featured John Cassavettes as a former jazz pianist turned private detective?

56. Who played Waldo, the owner of the club where Cassavettes hung out?

57. Who played Lucky Luciano on the premiere episode of "The Witness"?

58. What was the title of the early fifteen minute TV-series featuring real life New Jersey police sergeant Audley Walsh exposing various confidence games?

59. Where was Martin Kane's headquarters on the "Martin Kane, Private Eye" TV-series?

60. Who was the announcer for the series?

61. Who was Dr. Yat Su?

62. Who played the title role in the 1950s Dumont television series "The Plainclothesman"?

63. What was unusual about his performance?

64. "He's hard-boiled and dedicated to the proposition that crime does not pay. He's a man's man...but the ladies go for him too," read the commercial for his show. Who was he?

65. Who was the "champion of the people, defender of truth, guardian of our fundamental rights to life, liberty and the pursuit of happiness"?

66. In an early incarnation of the long-running TV-series "Dragnet," Sergeant Joe Friday, Badge 714, had a girl friend. Who played her?

67. Who played his fiancé in the 1967 series?

68. In "Jimmie Hughes, Rookie Cop," why did Jimmie (William Redfield) join the NYPD?

69. Who was the first actor to play James Bond?

70. Who played his nemesis Le Chiffre?

71. Who played the title role in "Police Woman Decoy"?

72. What was Nick Charles's, *The Thin Man,* former occupation?

73. What did the M stand for in "M Squad"?

74. What was the title of the last Perry Mason episode (telecast on September 4, 1966?)

75. Who played the judge in this episode?

76. What part did Paul Birch play on *"The Court of Last Resort"*?

77. Where was the detectives' headquarters located on "Hawaiian Eye"?

78. With what band did Cricket (Connie Stevens) sing?

79. Who played Hawaiian cabbie Kazuo Kim?

80. What was special about the title character in "A. Dunsten Lowell"?

81. Who played him?

82. In the short-lived TV-series "Cain's Hundred," criminal lawyer Nicholas Cain went undercover to infiltrate and ferret out the one hundred men who made up his own personal "most wanted" list (one per episode). Who played Cain?

83. How many men did he manage to bring to justice prior to the series' cancellation?

84. In "The Man from U.N.C.L.E.," what did UNCLE stand for?

85. What did their evil counterpart THRUSH stand for?

86. On "Mission: Impossible," who provided the voice on the tape that was played at the beginning of each episode (and would then self-destruct in five seconds)?

87. Where did Robert T. Ironside (Raymond Burr) reside on the TV-series "Ironside"?"

88. Mark Singer (Don Mitchell) was a young black man whom Ironside had arrested at one time, whom he later hired to be his "legs." During the later years of the series what did Mark do?

89. What was the collective title of the series that included "The Delphi Bureau," "Jigsaw," and "Assignment: Vienna" on a rotating basis?

90. In the TV-series "Banyon" how much did 1930s L.A. private detective Miles Banyon (Robert Forster) charge for his services?

91. What was Harry O's last name on "Harry-O"?

92. Why did Harry have to retire from the police force?

93. Where did Harry change his locale during his first season?

94. Who were his police contacts in each city?

95. Who wrote the screenplay for the 1974 TV-movie *Judge Dee and the Monastery Murder*?

96. What was the name of the character played by Jack Palance on the TV-series "Bronk"?

97. Who provided the voice of Charlie on "Charlie's Angels"?

98. On the PBS-series "Rumpole of the Bailey" what was the pet name Rumpole had for his wife?

99. What was her real name?

100. Who played her?

101. Who played Nero Wolfe in the TV-movie *The Doorbell Rang*?

102. On the TV-miniseries adaptation of Hammett's "The Dain Curse," the Continental Op (as played by James Coburn) had a name—what was it?

103. During the second season of "Remington Steele," Steele (Pierce Brosnan) and Laura Holt (Stephanie

Zimbalist) added a secretary named Mildred Krebbs (Doris Roberts) to their agency. How did they first make her acquaintance?

104. In what was possibly the most memorable cliff-hanger in television history—who shot J. R. Ewing on "Dallas"?

105. What was the title of the Edgar Award-winning pilot for the "Mike Hammer" TV-series starring Stacy Keach?

106. On "Hart to Hart," what was the name of Jonathan (Robert Wagner) and Jennifer's (Stefanie Powers) dog?

107. For what company did Banacek (George Peppard) usually work on the series "Banacek"?

108. Murray Matheson offered him research and advice on all of his cases. What was his character's name and occupation?

109. What were the names of the two pilots for the TV-series "Columbo"?

110. Who played the murderer in each one?

111. Peter Falk was not the original choice for the part of Columbo—who was?

112. Who played the title character in "Lanigan's Rabbi"?

113. What did police chief Paul Lanigan (Art Carney) do to collect his thoughts while working on a case?

114. What was the name of the TV-series that introduced McCloud (Dennis Weaver) on a semi-rotating basis with three other TV-series?

115. Where did McCloud originally come from?

116. What was his girl friend's name?

117. Who created the TV-series "Police Story"?

118. What was the title of the pilot for the "McMillan and Wife" series?

119. How did the character of Sally McMillan (Susan Saint James) leave the series?

120. What was Hal Holbrook's occupation in the TV-movie *Murder by Natural Causes?*

121. Who played his wife's lover with whom she was going to run away with after his death? (The wife was played by Katherine Ross.)

122. What was the setting of the "Hec Ramsey" TV-series starring Richard Boone?

123. What book provided the basis for the TV docu-drama *Murder in Texas?*

124. Who played the part of John Hill's (Sam Elliot's) murdered wife Joan?

125. Who played Joan's father, Ash Robinson?

126. What were the Snoop Sisters' (as played by Helen Hayes and Mildred Natwick) first names on "The Snoop Sisters"?

127. What part did Alan Alda play in the TV-movie *Kill Me If You Can?*

128. On *Dynasty* how did Adam Carrington hope to kill Jeff Colby?

Cases in History

For every fictional mystery put to paper, there are hundreds more crimes perpetrated in real life. Some have been utilized in classic plots of novels while other famous events have yielded legendary personalities whose notoriety has been gained through facts rather than through fictions.

1. Who established the Metropolitan Police Force of London in 1829?

2. What weapon did Lizzie Borden use to slay her parents?

3. How much was stolen in the famous Brinks' robbery that took place on January 17, 1950?

4. What was the name of the young boy who was kidnapped and murdered by Leopold and Loeb?

5. What did kidnapper/gangster George "Machine-Gun" Kelly say to the FBI agents who arrested him at gunpoint in 1946?

6. Who assassinated demagogue politician Huey "the Kingfish" Long?

7. Who stole the Mona Lisa on August 22, 1911?

8. Upon what case is "The Mystery of Marie Rogêt" actually based?

9. Who was convicted of the kidnapping/murder of the son of Charles Lindbergh?

10. Where did the great train robbery of August 8, 1963 take place?

11. What were the names of the two New York City cops who broke the famous "French Connection" case?

12. Who was "the Boston Strangler?"

13. Who was Dr. Sam Sheppard convicted of murdering?

14. What famous defense attorney helped him to get the decision reversed?

15. What was the name of the area of London menaced by Jack the Ripper?

16. Who murdered famed architect Stanford White?

17. What was the name of the "Lady in Red" who fingered John Dillinger to the FBI?

18. Who was the first "boss of bosses" of the Cosa Nostra?

19. What was the famous nickname of the thief who masterminded the theft of the Star of India?

20. What was the name of the family that was killed in cold blood by Richard Hickok and Perry Smith?

21. What was unusual about convicted sex murderer Richard Speck's chromosomal make-up?

22. What was the name of Charles Starkweather's girl friend who accompanied him on his killing spree? How old was she?

23. How did Mafia informant Joe Valachi die?

24. Who was the first person to be executed by electrocution?

25. Where did kidnappers Gary Steven Krist and Ruth Eisenmann-Schier hide their captive Barbara Jane Mackle in order to extort $500,000 from her father during the period of December 17–20, 1968?

The Murder of The Basking Family

On May 31, 1984, all ten members of the fabulously wealthy Basking family, ice-cream makers to the world, were viciously murdered. The county coroner, Dr. Jim Pastor, in cooperation with the investigating officers, has compiled the following list containing the ways in which each member of the family was killed. The murderer was undoubtably a mystery fanatic because the scenario for each murder resembles a scene taken from a murder mystery.

From what murder mystery is each scenario taken?

1. Rocky Basking (family patriarch)
   Poisoned by eating seven chocolate candies whose fillings were laced with nitro-benzene.

2. Frenchy Basking (Rocky's wife)
   Ingested lethal carbolic acid which had been substituted for her nightly drink of milk. The acid ate through her stomach wall.

3. Praline Basking (Rocky's sister)
   Bludgeoned to death by a "knock-em-dead" (a

hollow cow's tail filled with rocks and used like a blackjack).

4. Van Basking (Rocky's brother)
Stung by a poisonous strain of Italian bees who sting like hornets.

5. Choco Basking (Rocky's son)
Poisoned by ancient Borgia toxin contained in fifty miles of wire placed between the flock mattress and its satin casing. Poison was released when warmed by the body heat of the person reclining on the bed.

6. Spero Basking (Rocky's son)
Circulation stopped by the injection of an air bubble into a major artery.

7. Strawberry Basking (Rocky's daughter)
Died from a lethal snakebite (the snake is believed to have gained access to her bed via the bedroom bellrope that was formerly used to summon servants).

8. Peaches Basking (Rocky's daughter)
Death by suffocation (her entire body was painted gold).

9. Filbert Basking (Rocky's nephew)
Body badly broken and stuffed up a chimney.

10. Chip Basking (Rocky's grandson)
Shot through the heart while playing the piano (Rachmaninoff's Prelude in C Sharp Minor). Gun was triggered when Chip hit the soft pedal.

Who was the murderer?

The Masters' Quiz
...For
Experts Only

1. Who is Otto Penzler?

2. How did Dell Shannon derive her pseudonymous first name?

3. What is the address of the Mysterious Bookshop?

4. What is said to have occurred on Friday, January 6, 1854?

5. What was the number on Sam Spade's private investigator's license?

6. What was St. John Lord Merridew's most distinguishing facial feature?

7. Who lives at 24 St. Anne's Place, Greenwich Village, NYC?

8. What was Danny Williams academic background on "Hawaii Five-O?"

9. For what is the Robert L. Fish Award given each year by the Mystery Writer's of America?

10. What is *The Maul and the Pear Tree*?

ANSWERS

Humble Origins

1. Oedipus
2. Agamemnon
3. Clytemnestra (the queen) and Aegisthus (her lover)
4. Claudius
5. He poured poison into the king's ear.
6. King Duncan
7. Eleven
8. Bridget Allworthy
9. *Things as They Are*
10. Clithero Edring
11. Somnambulistic
12. C. Auguste Dupin
13. No. 33 Rue Dunot, Faubourg-St. Germain
14. "The Murders in the Rue Morgue"
15 "The Mystery of Marie Rogêt"

16. Monsieur Lecoq

17. Sherlock Holmes

18. Abel Magwitch, a convict

19. Inspector Bucket

20. Young Edwin Drood

21. John Jasper and Neville Landless

22. Wilkie Collins

23. Sergeant Cuff

24. Tending his roses

25. He stole a loaf of bread.

26. Ebenezer Gryce

27. It's the first detective novel written by a woman.

28. Through an analysis of a sample of the handwriting of both Hyde and Jekyll, Utterson, with the help of a handwriting expert, determines that both samples were written by the same person.

29. Sir Danvers Carew

30. A.J. Raffles

31. His friend, Bunny Manders

32. Fingerprint analysis

33. Arsène Lupin

34. Uncle Abner

35. He smokes a bhang pipe.

36. The Old Man in the Corner

37. Polly Burton

38. *The Evening Observer*

39. Doctor Christopher Jervis and Nathaniel Polton
40. 5a, King's Bench Walk

Sir Arthur Conan Doyle

1. Beeton's *Christmas Annual*
2. M. Dupin
3. Working as a ship's doctor on a whaler in the Arctic
4. *The Great Boer War*
5. The Fifth Northumberland Fusiliers
6. The Battle of Maiwand
7. Mary Morstan
8. Mrs. Martha Hudson
9. Sigerson is the identity Holmes used during his prolonged absences/disappearances.
10. Seven years
11. Irene Adler
12. *The Dynamics of an Asteroid*
13. "The Adventure of the Blanched Soldier" and "The Adventure of the Lion's Mane"
14. Reichenbach Falls in Switzerland
15. At a London hospital in their chemical laboratory
16. A plain gold wedding band

17. Revenge

18. Seven to five

19. Lestrade and Gregson

20. The Gasfitter's ball

21. Mr. Hardy

22. Alice

23. Her bridal bouquet

24. Miss Flora Miller

25. Blackmail

26. Jack Prendergast

27. Justice of the Peace Trevor

28. He used *baritsu*—a form of Japanese wrestling.

29. His brother Mycroft

30. Colonel Sebastian Moran

31. South African speculations

32. Yellow fever in South America

33. Dr. James Mortimer

34. Canada

35. One of his boots

36. Grimpen Mire

37. Jack and Beryl Stapleton, aka Mr. and Mrs. Vandeleur

38. Vermissa Valley

39. In his home, Sussex Manor House in Birlstone

40. Ted Baldwin

Agatha Christie

1. "Swallows Nest"
2. *The Black Arrow* owned by Alexander Parkinson
3. Iris Mullins, dressed as a man
4. A greenhouse converted into a storage room for toys
5. Inside the wooden rocking horse, Mathilda
6. Not being brother and sister
7. To set up a smokescreen to cover his crime
8. The governess, Elsie Holland
9. In an old deed box in his office –
10. Ladislous Malinovski
11. Lucerne, Switzerland, to a conference
12. Robert and Wilhelm Hoffman, international financiers
13. To insure her inheritance
14. Lady Hazy kept mistaking people for others that she knew.
15. Lady Bess Sedgewick
16. She had lived there briefly as a little girl.
17. Witnessing the murder

18. He was wearing surgical rubber gloves.

19. Jackie Afflick's

20. *The Duchess of Malfi*

21. Styles

22. *The Mysterious Affair at Styles* (1920) and *Curtain* (1975)

23. X ; Stephen Norton

24. He allows the Lord to decide his fate by leaving his heart medicine out of his own reach before going to bed on the night he has murdered Norton; he succumbs to a heart attack that·night.

25. Gardening

26. He is stabbed in the back.

27. Fernly Glen in the village of King's Abbot

28. Dr. Sheppard, the novel's narrator

29. The Tavrus Express

30. Because Poirot didn't like his (Ratchett's) face

31. "...member little Daisy Armstrong."

32. Cassetti, the infamous˙ American kidnapper

33. A is Alice Ascher of Andover; B is Betty Barnard of Bexhill and C is Carmichael Clarke of Churston

34. George Earlsfield

35. Mystery writer; apple addict

36. Joyce Reynolds

37. Mrs. Rowena Drake

38. *Cards on the Table* (1936), *Mrs. McGinty's Dead* (1952), *Dead Man's Folly* (1956), *Third Girl* (1961), and *Elephants Can Remember* (1972)

39. Arthur Hastings

40. "Something's Afoot"; *Ten Little Indians* (1939)

Raymond Chandler

1. Quarter of a million dollars

2. From Paul Marsten during World War II

3. Paul Edward Marsten

4. She killed her husband and Sylvia Lennox.

5. Mrs. Loring's chauffeur

6. They were sisters.

7. Señor Maioranos

8. Christopher Lavery

9. Little Faun Lake

10. Muriel Chess

11. Degarmo knew it was a blackjack that Marlowe was hit with.

12. They had once been lovers.

13. Miss Gromsett

14. The Indian Head Hotel

15. Little Velma Valento

16. Florian's

17. Purissima Canyon

18. Red Norgaard
19. Fei-tsui jade
20. Owner of the Belvedere Club

John Creasey

1. Fatalis, a deadly ore

2. He had a natural immunity to "fatalis."

3. Banister's girl friend was the professor's niece.

4. Antarctica; Anak is the leader.

5. High Peak

6. Kate McGuire left it there.

7. He and his friends find the baby's mother.

8. She took the records naming everyone involved in the stolen goods racket.

9. Gabby the Trainer

10. Ossy Osgood

11. His aunt, Lady Hurst, introduced him to her.

12. Madame Melinska

13. His trophy wall

14. She interrupted two thieves in the act of stealing her jewels.

15. The baby's uncle

16. The impersonator had the wrong hairstyle.
17. Rake Hunter, international criminal
18. Superintendent Partridge
19. Royal Automobile Club
20. Lieutenant Maria Consuela

Mignon G. Eberhart

1. The Golden Spike Rail
2. In her attaché case
3. Rhoda's letters to Guy Casso
4. Walter Banner
5. For blackmailing Marsh and Banner
6. An author published by Esseven's company
7. She wanted her husband to sell the family publishing business.
8. Six million dollars
9. Give Mr. Bronson an alibi for the time of the murder
10. She had seen him at the murder scene, and thus could incriminate him.
11. Near the edge of the Westchester Airport
12. John Nelson

13. Nelson had been a teller in Clanser's bank.

14. Cat hairs on his clothes

15. Boxing; his nickname was Pretty-Boy.

16. Sarah Keate

17. He said he knew a friend of Craig Brent's.

18. He mistook him for Peter Huber.

19. Anna Haub, the maid

20. They were sister and brother.

Dick Francis

1. Photographs of blackmail letters to certain horse owners and trainers

2. He "suggested" they donate large sums of money to the Injured Jockeys Fund.

3. Drug pusher Lance Kinship

4. He would inherit one hundred thousand pounds if he would find his stepsister, Amanda.

5. *Horse and Hound*

6. Swine *erysipelas,* a disease peculiar to pigs

7. Trevor Deansgate, the bookie

8. Tri-Nitro

9. Research into Coronary Disability

10. Norris Abbott, the con man

11. Wax polish for antique furniture

12. His soul and his column

13. Misleading information about the horses expected to be winners

14. At Norton Fox's stable

15. Vjoesterod, a South African bookmaker

16. Ascot Racetrack

17. Selenium

18. It was inside the apples they ate.

19. Pen Warner

20. She overheard the criminals discussing their crimes.

Erle Stanley Gardner

1. Sidney Enversel, Mrs. Wentworth's lover

2. A second place medal in the women's tennis tournament

3. He had scorned her.

4. Emil Scanlon.

5. With evidence that she was an expert long-distance swimmer.

6. Steer Ridge Oil and Refining

7. Fred Hedley, her fiancé

8. He was a blackmailer.

9. He heard a gunshot around nine o'clock on the night of the murder.

10. Near the seventh hole on the golf course

11. Butte Valley Guest Ranch

12. Faith Collision

13. Nurse Melita Doon

14. He posed as an encyclopedia salesman.

15. Dolores Ferrol

16. Jarvis C. Archer, her employer

17. Pauline Garson

18. They were partners in blackmail.

19. Pint-size

20. Family friend and executor of Boxter C. Gillett's will

Dashiell Hammett

1. *Black Mask*

2. Just as the Op himself, the boss is nameless. He is referred to as "the Old Man."

3. Personville, pronounced Poisonville

4. Donald Willsson

5. Publisher of the *Morning* and *Evening Herald*

6. Mining

7. A lineage of corruption and addiction

8. To locate some missing diamonds that had last been in the custody of the Leggett family.

9. The Temple of the Holy Grail

10. Miles Archer

11. The Fat Man

12. Effie Perrine

13. "She's a knockout."

14. $5000

15. One one-thousand dollar bill

16. Greek

17. The Trans-American Detective Agency

18. Schnauzer

19. The Normandie Hotel

20. A .32 caliber gun

BONUS—**Clyde Miller Wynant**

P. D. James

1. Phyllis Dorothy

2. From Detective-Commander to Detective-Chief Inspector

3. Atypical mononucleosis; leukemia

4. Working in an unofficial capacity

5. The Honjohn

6. Attending a party celebrating the third reprint of his first book of poetry

7. The Steen Clinic in London

8. Stabbed through the heart with a chisel

9. Monksmere

10. Maurice Seton

11. The Cluch Pit murder case

12. Bludgeoned to death with a heavy mallet

13. Brenda Pridmore

14. Itinerant Marxist poet and amateur revolutionary

15. She was sent to a convent school despite the fact that she was a Protestant.

16. Pryde's Detective Agency

17. Sir Roland Callendar

18. A small bouquet of wildflowers

19. Courcy Island off the Dorset Coast

20. *The Duchess of Malfi*

Peter Lovesey

1. Millie

2. Edward

3. The Charles Pearce case in 1878

4. Sir Charles Warren

5. Inspector Jowett

6. A "wobble" also known as a "go as you please contest," was a six-day race, usually held on an enclosed circular track, where runners were allowed to set their own pace with the intention of covering the largest amount of distance.

7. Charles Darrell and Captain Erskine Chadwick

8. First prize—a belt worth £100 and £500 cash; second prize—£100; and third prize £50

9. Strychnine poisoning (strychnine, though toxic, can also be used as a stimulant).

10. Captain Erskine Caldwell—538 miles

11. *The Detective Wore Silk Drawers* (1971)

12. Miriam Cromer

13. The public hangman

14. A photograph cut out from a magazine that depicted the woman's husband and another man.

15. Josiah Perceval; poisoned with potassium cyanide

16. Madame Tussaud's Wax Museum where Berry will sell the clothes that Miriam wore at her execution so that they may be used in an execution tableau.

17. A Royal Worcester vase in the Japanese style

18. Peter Brown

19. The Royal Society

20. Brighton

Ed McBain

1. Volkswagon Beetle

2. At the A & M Exxon station

3. The "Kitty Corner"

4. One of her paintings

5. The state's attorney

6. "Frenzy"

7. Charles Hoggs

8. Illustrating children's books

9. Mary Gibson

10. Disown both Vicky and her daughter Allison

11. The Beverly Wilshire

12. So the police would have trouble determining the time of Newman's death.

13. Larry Patterson

14. Ruger .44 caliber Magnum Blackhawk

15. Her psychiatrist, Dr. James Brolin

16. Strophanthin

17. Treated the capsule with a one-percent solution of formaldehyde

18. "Cookie"

19. Assistant to the company psychologist

20. Performed an autopsy on a celebrity

John D. MacDonald

1. The Church of the Apocrypha

2. Brother Titus

3. Thomas McGraw—a man in search of his daughter

4. Bobbi Jo Annison, ex-evangelist

5. International terrorism

6. Sapphires and rubies

7. He shared a cell in Leavenworth with Cathy's father.

8. Alabama Tiger

9. At Harry's in New York

10. Lois Atkinson

11. A lobotomy was performed on him.

12. Rossa dropped Daska-15 into his drink.

13. Varn, Moore, and Daska

14. He loaded the coffee urn in the cafeteria with drugs.

15. Baynard Mulligan, Armister's lawyer

16. The *Buccaneer*

17. Mildred Mooney

18. $250,000

19. TV technicians

20. The Rod-and-Gun Club

Ross Macdonald

1. Kenneth Millar

2. To avoid confusion with his wife, fellow mystery writer Margaret Millar

3. John Ross Macdonald

4. June 2, 1914

5. Hugh Western

6. The Philippines during World War II

7. A bearded nude painted by Western

8. Burke Damis

9. Quincy Ralph Simpson

10. Bruce Campion

11. Harriet Blackwell

12. The Laguna Perdida School

13. Tom Hillman

14. The Barcelona Hotel

15. The murderer, Mrs. Hillman, commits suicide by piercing her chest with steel knitting needles. She died the next day.

16. It is mentioned only once. It refers to the fate awaiting the flesh peddlers and all others living in pursuit of the rapid buck. Death waits on the far side of the last dollar.

17. Lieutenant Bret Taylor

18. Howard Cross

19. Bourke

20. These two films (the first and second in Paul Newman's Harper series) are based on the first two Archer novels—*The Moving Target* (1949) and *The Drowning Pool* (1950).

BONUS—**"I'm not Archer, exactly, but Archer is me."**

Ngaio Marsh

1. Rachmaninoff's *Prelude* in C-Sharp Minor
2. Georgie Biggens
3. By putting her left foot down on the soft pedal of the piano
4. To make herself cry
5. Jealousy
6. Dr. Basil Schramm
7. He tried to blackmail Mrs. Foster's killer.
8. Carter was blackmailing her.
9. Inspector Alleyn's wife
10. In Carter's breast pocket when he was buried
11. She knew her favorite son was a murderer.
12. Nicholas Compline
13. He rigged up a fishing line and trout fly.
14. In Mrs. Compline's hat
15. She wrote a letter intimating that she was the killer.
16. He threatened to expose Grant as an alleged plagiarist.

17. A list of the key figures in the drug rackets

18. He was thrown down a well.

19. Baron Van der Veghel

20. The killer was missing from the group picture.

Ellery Queen

1. Inportuna agreed not to prosecute her father for embezzlement.

2. He changed his birthdate.

3. Virginia's diary note of lunch with Peter on December 9

4. "Newborn Child Emerging"

5. Edward Lloyd Merkenthaler, business scout for Nino Inportuna

6. They were all anagrams for Mona Lisa.

7. Diedrich Van Horn

8. A commission for his son Howard

9. In the false bottom of Sally's jewelry case

10. He had the serial numbers of the money paid to the blackmailer.

11. All were typed in red ink.

12. They arranged a code using a New York guidebook.

13. Her husband Dirk, before their marriage

14. George T. Johnson

15. He had been double-crossed.

16. The United States Government "suggested" they do it.

17. Karla, his wife

18. It was hidden in the false bottom of a bottle of cognac.

19. Judah, his other brother

20. Colonel Spring

Dorothy L. Sayers

1. Eton and Balliol College

2. "As my whimsy takes me."

3. It is never mentioned.

4. Lord Peter was a captain; Bunter a sergeant.

5. The way he brews coffee

6. Harriet Vane; a mystery writer

7. In a bathtub

8. It is naked save for a pair of gold pince-nez.

9. Mr. Campbell, a landscape painter

10. Kirkcudbright Galloway

11. To fish

12. *Suspicious Characters*

13. Pym's Publicity, Ltd.

14. Victor Dean

15. A broken neck, possibly caused by a fall down the stairs

16. Mr. Death Bredon

17. "Advertise, or go under."

18. Fenchurch St. Paul

19. Nine hours

20. The face was mutilated and the hands were cut off at the wrists.

BONUS—*Changes Rung on an Old Theme in Two Short Touches and Two Full Peals*

Dell Shannon

1. Elizabeth Linington

2. Alison Weir Mendoza

3. John Luis and Teresa Ann

4. Father O'Brien; a rare antique silver cross

5. He left his wheelchair behind.

6. Mr. Yaeger

7. Sergeant Walt Robsen

8. Hollenbeck precinct

9. They were all apparently beaten to death.

10. The County Museum of Natural History on a field trip with her school

11. Gustave L. Snyder

12. Luisa May

13. Rosalie Ybarra

14. St. Ignacio's parish school

15. She was a reputed white witch.

16. The British Isles

17. Wonderful (He made the plans without his wife's knowledge.)

18. Jeanne Martin

19. Ruth Hoffman

20. France

Georges Simenon

1. Jules

2. The estate de Saint-Fiacre where his father worked

3. On the Quai des Orfevres

4. Evariste

5. All Souls' Day

6. A falsified newspaper clipping concerning the apparent suicide of the Comte de Saint-Fiacre

7. Maurice de Saint-Fiacre

8. Ernest

9. Nine Moinard

10. Roger Couchet

11. He was an ether addict.

12. One-third to his first wife, one-third to his second wife, and one-third to his mistress. The will was to be contested by both wives.

13. Morals charges claiming that Maigret got a young lady intoxicated and took advantage of her in a shady hotel.

14. The girl's uncle, Monsieur Jean-Baptiste Prieur

15. Madame de Carame

16. "I'm relying on you; I trust you."

17. Suffocation

18. His fingernails were perfectly manicured.

19. La Baule

20. Jean Dollent

BONUS: *Intimate Memoirs: Including Marie-Jo's Book* **(1984)**

Mickey Spillane

1. Frank Morrison Spillane

2. Velda

3. Pat Chambers

4. *I, the Jury*

5. Jack Williams

6. Shot in the stomach with a dum-dum bullet

7. Death in the same manner as his friend had died

8. "It was easy," I said. (In response to the question, "How could you?")

9. Nancy Sanford

10. Mike Hammer, via his old address thanking him for his caring

11. "Your Redhead."

12. He was still screaming when I pulled the trigger.

13. Chester Wheeler

14. Juno was a queen, all right, a real live queen. You know the kind. *Juno was a man.*

15. Tiger Mann

16. Ryan

17. He attended college for two years.

18. Customers (He deplores the word "fans.")

19. *The Girl Hunters* (1973)

20. *The Erection Set* (1972).

BONUS—**A science-fiction/suspense story by Spillane that was published in *Fantastic* in 1952**

Rex Stout

1. A brownstone on West 35th Street (The house number has been inconsistent throughout the course of the novels).

2. Fritz Brenner—the cook/majordomo of the household; and Theodore Horstmann—who tends Wolfe's top floor greehouse/conservatory

3. Saul Panzer, Fred Durkin, and Orrie Cather

4. Remmers (followed closely by his own home brew)

5. Billiards (followed closely by crossword puzzles and cribbage)

6. He plays darts (which he calls javelins) for fifteen minutes each day.

7. The Metropolitan Orchid Show

8. "X," or as he is more properly known, Arnold Zeck

9. It has never been revealed and neither of them are willing to talk about it.

10. *Fer-de-Lance* (1934)

11. A poisonous snake

12. Isabel Kerr

13. *Death of a Dude* (1969)

14. The League of Atonement

15. J. Edgar Hoover

16. That Watson was a woman

17. *Double for Death* (1939)

18. It featured another Stout creation—Tecumseh Fox instead of Nero Wolfe.

19. "...it is only a catastrophe."

20. "...those you have yourself forgotten."

BONUS—**Marko Vukcic**

CLERICAL MYSTERIES

Gilbert Keith Chesterton

1. The close friendship/philosophical kinship between Chesterton and the poet Hilaire Belloc

2. Father John O'Connor

3. Paradox

4. Dr. Orion Hood

5. Zaladin, the magician

6. Colonel Dubosc was Dr. Hirsch in disguise.

7. Duc de Velognes

8. The formula for the new noiseless powder

William Kienzle

1. All were priests and nuns.

2. It was the symbol of death.

3. The Ten Commandments

4. Inspector Walter Koznicki; his partner was Lieutenant Ned Harris.

5. Heart failure

6. A voodoo priestess

7. Roman Toussaint

8. On Cardinal Mooney's tomb

9. Monsignor Thompson's diary

10. Pat Lennon of the *Detroit News* and Joe Cox of the *Detroit Free Press*

11. He "killed" Monsignor Thompson's reputation.

12. The *Alaskan Queen*

Harry Kemelman

1. The victim's handbag

2. The Serafino family

3. Lie about the time he took her home

4. Officer Bill Norman

5. The Surfside Restaurant

6. Green was Jordon's illegitimate son.

7. He knew that Jordon was dead and would not see it.

8. Lawrence Gore did it to inherit Jordon's fortune.

9. To obscure the fact he was an expert marksman.

10. The killer left his fingerprint on the key used to wind the carriage clock.

THOSE INSCRUTABLE ORIENTALS

John P. Marquand

1. Casey Lee
2. The secret aviation-fuel formula
3. He wanted to close down a gambling house.
4. The Chinese rebels
5. Jack Rhyce and Ruth Bogart
6. Working as undercover agents for the United States

Robert Van Gulik

7. A one-armed naked lady
8. A poultice of orange peels
9. To investigate the death of the old Abbot

10. In the Gallery of Horrors
11 A counsellor of the Beggar's Guild
12. He was to be drawn and quartered.
13. He was a highwayman.

Earl Derr Biggers

14. Mr. Kashimo
15. The *President Arthur*
16. A camera strap
17. In the cuff of his right pants leg
18. Jimmy Bradshaw's
19. They were brothers.
20. Denny Mayo's name was inscribed in it.

The Medical Mysteries of Robin Cook

1. Michelle was inhaling benzene from the pond behind her playhouse.

2. The same people who owned the Weinberger Cancer Institute

3. Hundred-pound sacks of potatoes

4. Concussion grenades

5. Wally Crab

6. Sudden Surgical Death

7. From a drug overdose in their IVs

8. He ordered from out-of-state drug firms using deceased doctors' names.

9. She smelled his Yves St. Laurent Cologne.

10. Andrea Bryant

THE NEW HARD-BOILED AND TONGUE-IN-CHEEK MYSTERIES

Stuart Kaminsky

1. He was a cop on the Glendale police force, and then a security guard at Warner Brothers.

2. He's a lieutenant for the LAPD homicide division.

3. A dentist named Shelly Minck

4. Raymond Chandler

Robert B. Parker

5. The Korean Conflict

6. Stuart Street, second floor front (a half block down from Treemont)

7. *The Goldwulf Manuscript* (1973)

8. University President Bradford W. Forbes, then Roland Orchard, and then Terry Orchard

9. *Promised Land* (1976)

10. They had trained and had boxed together on the same fight card during their early years.

11. London

12. April Kyle

Bill Pronzini

13. He doesn't have one; he is known as "the Nameless Detective."
14. San Francisco

Jack Lynch

15. Armando Barker
16. Sand Valley

Elmore Leonard

17. Ernest Stickly, Jr.
18. Rene Moya

19. *Swag* (1976), formerly called *Ryan's Rules*
20. Joey LaBrava

Roger L. Simon

21. He was a Berkeley dropout.
22. Aunt Sonya
23. *Rip It Off* (Simon's self-conscious parallel to *Steal This Book* by Abbie Hoffman.)
24. Cottonwood Meadows
25. Governor Dillworthy
26. Miles Hawthorne
27. *Murder on the Orient Express* meets the Bamboo Curtain
28. Chairman Mao's favorite private eye

Gregory Mcdonald

29. Irwin Maurice Fletcher
30. *News-Tribune*

31. He will pay Fletch a thousand dollars if Fletch will murder him.

32. Candidate for the presidency, Caxton Wheeler

33. Francis Xavier Flynn

34. An inspector on the Boston police force

35. Ada, Texas, Frampton, Massachusetts, and the Pentagon

36. The president of the United States (only as a security drill)

Daniel Odier

37. In one, an exclusive "bootleg" recording of a renowned diva who refused to have her voice recorded, and in the other, police evidence against an organized crime kingpin.

38. Cynthia Hawkins

39. Gorodish was about forty, and Alba was thirteen.

40. Delacorta

Mini-Mysteries:
The Short Story

1. "The Mystery of a Hansom Cab" by Fergus Hume
2. "A Retrieved Reformation" by O. Henry
3. Dr. Edgar Beaumont
4. J. E. Murddock
5. The wedding of Sydney Harcourt and Lillian Ray
6. Paul Beck
7. Carnacki (the Ghost Finder)
8. No. 472 Cheyne Walk, Chelsea
9. Dodgson, Arkright, Jessop, and Taylor
10. Dinner at Carnacki's house
11. A haunted sailing ship, featured in the short story "The Haunted *Jarvee*"
12. Professor Augustus S. F. X. van Dusen
13. Dr. Ransome and Alfred Fielding
14. Chisolm prison
15. Two tens and one five dollar bill, tooth powder, and a new shine and polish for his shoes (He later also requested a bowl of water to sate his thirst each night.)

16. Nicky Welt

17. English literature

18. *The Nine Mile Walk* (1967)

19. Welt's chess-mate, the District Attorney of Suffolk County, Mass.

20. Samuel Johnson and James Boswell

BONUS—**Lillian Bueno**

Whodunit?

1. A false clue

2. In seventeenth century England anti-hunt people used an odorous, smoked (reddish colored) herring to draw the dogs off the scent of the fox.

3. Harvey and Jeanette Crewe

4. The murdered woman's father Len Dembar.

5. Bloodstains throughout the house and a baby in a crib

6. The Sheepherder's Association

7. Inspector Bruce Hubbell

8. Arthur Thomas

9. They planted evidence on the accused man's property.

10. R. D. Muldoon

Based on Fact

1. The Leopold and Loeb case/trial
2. The Starkweather-Fugate killing spree
3. The Gary Gilmore case/trial/execution
4. The Rosenbergs espionage trial
5. The Leopold and Loeb case
6. The Sacco and Vanzetti case/trial
7. The Edward Gein case
8. Richard III's murderous ascension to the throne
9. The Hickock-Perry case/trial/execution
10. The murder of Kitty Genovese

Surprise Mystery Authors

1. Gavin Stephens
2. A lawyer

3. Freelance press agent

4. Gore Vidal

5. Antony Gillingham

6. Jemima Shaw

7. Blessed Eleanor's Convent of the Community of the Order of the Tower of Ivory

8. Henry Jacobson

9. The name was withheld.

10. Devores was fastidious to a fault and would never have left his clothes strewn around the room as they were at the scene of his demise.

11. He was an ex-prizefighter in the light heavyweight division.

12. Lamour was also a prizefighter at one time in his life.

13. *The House of Shade*

14. *Death Is a Lonely Business*

15. Xavier Kilgarvan

16. "The Bloodstained Bridal Gown"

17. Toni Tennille

18. Roger Dale

19. Brother William of Baskerville

20. Franciscan

Whodunit II

1. Bill Norman (*Friday the Rabbi Slept Late*)
2. Jonathan Brewster (*Arsenic and Old Lace*)
3. Bernie Pryde (*An Unsuitable Job for a Woman*)—he committed suicide.
4. Manuel Kimball (*Fer-de-Lance*)
5. James Berry (*Waxwork*)
6. Brigid O'Shaughnessy (*The Maltese Falcon*)
7. Hercule Poirot (*Curtain*)
8. Jack McCall
9. Hazel Tooms (*The Case of the Postponed Murder*)
10. Jefferson Hope (*A Study in Scarlet*)

NEW TALENT

Liza Cody

1. Corroded metal
2. Film piracy
3. At the film laboratory
4. To prevent her father testifying against murderer Willy Dutch
5. Davey Spoon and Bessie at the Half-Moon
6. Shake, Rattle, and Roll
7. Brierly Security

Karin Berne

8. A pair of diamond earrings
9. She hit him with a pot of chile.
10. Sell it to reporter Steve Tedesco

Nathan Aldyne

11. Bonaparte's
12. Billy Golacinsky
13. Lieutenant William Searcy
14. A shade of red lipstick that was the color of the stain on the murdered hustler's handkerchief
15. Provincetown

Bill Adler and Thomas Chastain

16. *Who Killed the Robins Family? ... And Where and When and How and Why Did They Die?*
17. Nine
18. Tyler, Evelyn, Marshall, Libby, Lewis, James, Cynthia, Candace, and Pamela
19. Libby; her last name is Pittman.
20. Alfred Wales

Radio

1. Carlton E. Morse
2. "No job too tough, no mystery too baffling."
3. Barton Yorborough
4. Two hundred thirty-nine pounds
5. Ed Begley
6. Agnes Moorehead
7. How to cloud men's minds so they could not see him
8. The weed of crime
9. Newsman
10. The *Star-Times*
11. Edmund O'Brien
12. "This crazy life"
13. Bernie Surrey
14. Lucille Fletcher
15. Agnes Moorehead
16. Lon Clark
17. Secretary Patsy Bowen was played by actress Helen Choate
18. Lurene Tuttle

19. "How much money you got on you?"

20. San Francisco

21. Richard Denning and Barbara Britton

22. Cabbie Mahatma McGloin was played by actor Mandel Kramer.

23. Wally Maher

24. Brett Halliday

25. As "fiction's most famous criminal lawyer"

26. Frank Lovejoy

27. William Gillette as Holmes and Leigh Lovell as Dr. Watson

28. A cup of George Washington coffee

29. Orson Welles

30. *Ruddigore.*

ON THE STAGE

John Pielmeir

1. Elizabeth Ashley

2. She feared she would not be able to squeeze into heaven.

3. Amanda Plummer
4. Singing

Ira Levin

5. John Wood and Marion Seldes
6. Needlepoint
7. The hearth rug

Robert Marasco

8. Dodge ball
9. Joe Dobbs played by actor Pat Hingle
10. He made malicious phone calls to Mr. Malley's (Fritz Weaver) house.

Anthony Shaffer

11. A ruby necklace
12. St. John Lord Merridew
13. In the clock

W. Somerset Maugham

14. The Chinese Woman (Lady Ching Goe)
15. Katherine Cornell
16. Sumatra
17. She made a lace collar for the prison matron, Mrs. Parker (Mary Scott Seton).

Agatha Christie

18. Gene Lyons
19. Janet MacKenzie, the housekeeper
20. One

At the Movies

1. Spies on neighbors with binoculars and telescopic camera lens
2. Raymond Burr
3. Lars Thorwald
4. She was his housekeeper.
5. Burt Lancaster
6. He needed her insurance money to pay off some drug dealers.
7. Her illness was psychosomatic and she could be cured.
8. Dr. Alexander, Leona's physician

9. Audrey Totter and Hurd Hatfield

10. To investigate the mysterious suicide of Victor's secretary

11. Matilda Frazier

12. Victor had cut the brakelines

13. Samantha Jones

14. He pretends to be a cop.

15. Inside the doll Sam gave to his wife Susie

16. Richard Crenna

17. Ronald Colman

18. Claud Allister

19. John Barrymore

20. *Calling Bulldog Drummond*

21. Joan Bennett

22. Heidt was blackmailing him.

23. Criminal Psychology

24. Professor Wanley was dreaming.

25. Sam, Jack's boss

26. He was recording wind-sounds for a movie soundtrack.

27. John Lithgow

28. *Co-ed Frenzy*

29. Norman poisoned her with strychnine.

30. John McIntyre and Lurene Tuttle

31. Marian's lover, Sam Loomis

32. Hershey's chocolate syrup

33. Jacobi
34. Baseball
35. Dorothy Adams
36. In the clock in Laura's apartment
37. Actor Walter Huston was director John Huston's father.
38. Gardenia
39. Elisha Cook, Jr.
40. Ricardo Cortez
41. Lucille Watson and Harry Davenport
42. *After The Thin Man* (1936)
43. *Another Thin Man* (1939)
44. Dashiell Hammett
45. Alec Guinness
46. St. Augustine's cross
47. Raymond Chandler and James Cain
48. Walter Neff, the insurance salesman
49. Phyllis Dietrichson
50. Edward G. Robinson
51. Ralph Bellamy
52. Margaret Lindsay
53. Charles Grapewin
54. Michael Crichton
55. Genevieve Bujold
56. The Jefferson Institute
57. Tom Selleck

58. A "clearing house" for transplant organs

59. Fred Weber and Angie Dickinson

60. Philadelphia Museum of Art

61. Teenager Peter Miller

62. Michael Caine

63. Prasada

64. Michael Biehn

65. Belle Goldman

66. He slashes Sally's portrait.

67. "Never Say Never"

68. Duke Ellington

69. Murdering the man who raped his wife Laura

70. Eve Arden and Brooks West

71. Irresistible impulse

72. Mary knew that Laura's ripped panties were in the laundry chute of her father's hotel.

73. Judge Weaver

74. Elderberry wine laced with arsenic, cyanide, and strychnine

75. Victim number 12

76. Peter Lorre

77. Yellow fever

78. Edward Everett Horton

79. A cat steps on the fuse box and all the lights go out.

80. Frank and Cora rig an auto accident.

81. The $10,000 insurance payment

82. John Colicos

83. Bill Macy

84. Her former lover, Brian

85. Howard Duff

86. Lew Ayres

87. Salesgirl at a newstand

88. She fakes a suicide.

89. Thomas Mitchell

90. Louis Bernard was played by actor Daniel Gelen.

91. Someone would be assassinated

92. *Que Sera, Sera*

93. Jo McKenna

94. Reggie Nalder

95. Duke

96. $150,000

97. William Bendix

98. Mexico

99. He is an avid reader of pulp mystery stories.

100. Macdonald Carey

101. A ring that belonged to one of his victims

102. He locks her in the garage with the car running.

103. Roman Polanski

104. Adolphe Menjou

105. Noah Cross, played by John Huston

106. Perry Lopez

107. He was a cop.

108. Gus Saltic

109. Thirty

110. Richard Castellano

111. Kim Novak

112. Turn-of-the-century belle, Carlotta

113. San Juan Batista

114. James Stewart

115. He finds Madelaine's jewelry in Judy's dresser.

116. Doghouse Riley

117. Dorothy Malone

118. Packard

119. Blackmailer Joe Brady

120. Mrs. Vivian Ruthledge

On Television

1. It was Keye Luke who had played Charlie's Number One Son in several of the 1930s films.

2. Half of the show was spent catching the crook, and the other half was spent convicting him.

3. "The Forget-Me-Knot" (June 20, 1968)

4. Patrick Newell

5. Lieutenant Shiller (Dana Eclar) and Lieutenant Hal Brubaker (Edward Grover)

6. The King Edward Hotel

7. Los Angeles 53rd Precinct

8. To find his son's killer

9. Nichols, Darell, and Darell

10. Kent Taylor

11. "Amos Burke, Secret Agent"

12. J. Carrol Naish; James Hong

13. Barry

14. Sebastion Cabot as Dr. Carl Hyatt

15. Dick Powell

16. "Danger Man"

17. "To Kill a Cop"

18. P.C.

19. The one-armed man

20. Bill Raisch as Fred Johnson.

21. "Mrs. Columbo," "Kate Columbo," "Kate the Detective," and "Kate Loves a Mystery"

22. *The Weekly Advertiser*

23. Jenny played by Lili Hayden

24. Samuel Bennett as played by Patrick O'Neal

25. "Khan!"

26. "The Marcus-Nelson Murders," based on the Wylie-Hoffert murder case.

27. It was the name used by George Savalas (Telly's

brother) as his billing for the part of Detective Stavros on "Kojak."

28. "The Lawless Years" which preceded "The Untouchables" by a half of a season

29. "Streets of Danger"

30. The Great Pacific Casualty Company

31. A booby-trapped bottle of champagne exploded, killing his wife and blinding him on their wedding night.

32. Pax

33. He didn't carry a gun.

34. Robert Preston

35. Richard Denning

36. A publisher

37. Henry Mancini

38. 351 Ellis Park Road

39. Hope Emerson and Minerva Urecal

40. David Ross.

41. Robert Vaughn as Harry Rule

42. John S. Ragin as Dr. Robert J. Asten

43. Danny's Place

44. Mary Tyler Moore and Roxanne Brooks

45. Her legs (They were the only thing the audience ever saw.)

46. Barbara Bain as Karen Wells

47. "Call Mr. D"

48. Steve Bochco, who later went on to create "Hill Street Blues."

49. "School's Out"

50. Suzanne Pleshette, as an amnesiac in the series pilot "Richie Brockelman: The Missing 24 Hours."

51. Jim Rockford (James Garner)

52. Dino's Lodge

53. Gerald Lloyd Kookson III, aka "Kookie," the parking-lot attendant played by Edd Byrnes

54. "Shaft"

55. "Staccato"

56. Eduardo Ciannelli

57. Telly Savalas

58. "Rackets Are My Racket"

59. Happy McMann's Tobacco Shop

60. Walter Cronkite

61. A San Francisco Chinatown shopowner/amateur detective played by Marvin Miller in "Mysteries of Chinatown"

62. Ken Lynch

63. Since the entire series was shot from his point of view, his character was only seen when he looked in the mirror or vis-à-vis in a flashback.

64. Charlie Wild on the TV-series "Charlie Wild: Private Eye"

65. "Mr. District Attorney" as played by Jay Jostyn

66. Marjie Miller

67. Dorothy Abbott

68. To find his father's killer (His bloodlust is cured by the camraderie of his fellow cops and the morality of their code of honor.)

69. Barry Nelson on the "Casino Royale" episode of "Climax"

70. Peter Lorre

71. Beverly Garland as officer Casey Jones.

72. Operative of the Trans-American Detective Agency

73. Murder

74. "The Case of the Final Fade-out"

75. Author Erle Stanley Gardner

76. Author/attorney Erle Stanley Gardner

77. The Hawaiian Village Hotel

78. The Arthur Lyman Band

79. Poncie Ponce

80. He was a detective with ESP.

81. Robert Vaughn

82. Mark Richman

83. Thirty

84. United Network Command for Law and Enforcement

85. Initially, it was never meant as an acronym, but at the suggestion of a member of the U.N.C.L.E. fan club it came to mean Technological Hierarchy for the Removal of Undesirables and the Subjugation of Humanity.

86. Bob Johnson

87. The attic of police headquarters

88. He went to law school and became a lawyer.

89. "The Men"

90. Twenty bucks a day

91. Orwell

92. He was shot in the back and the bullet was inoperable due to its proximity to his spine.

93. From San Diego to Los Angeles

94. Detective Manny Quinlan of the San Diego Police Force as played by Henry Darrow; Lieutenant K. C. Trench of the Los Angeles Police Force as played by Anthony Zerbe.

95. Nicholas Meyers

96. Lieutenant Alexander Bronkov.

97. John Forsythe

98. "She Who Must Be Obeyed"

99. Hilda

100. Peggy Thorpe-Bates

101. Thayer David

102. Hamilton Nashe

103. She was an IRS agent who came to audit the Remington Steele Agency.

104. Kristin Sheppard as played by Mary Francis Crosby

105. "Mickey Spillane's Mike Hammer in Murder Me Murder You"

106. Freeway

107. Boston Casualty

108. Felix Mullholland, owner of Mullholland's Rare Book and Print Shop

109. "Prescription: Murder" and "Ransom for a Dead Man"

110. Gene Barry; Lee Grant

111. Bing Crosby

112. The part of Rabbi David Small was played by Stuart Margolin in the pilot and by Bruce Solomon on the series.

113. He'd play the piano and sing along with himself to the song "One Hundred Bottles of Beer on the Wall."

114. "Four-in-One"

115. Taos, New Mexico

116. Chris Coughlin as played by Diane Muldaur

117. Joseph Wambaugh

118. "Once Upon a Dead Man"

119. She died in a plane crash.

120. Mentalist

121. Richard Anderson (She double-crossed her other lover Barry Botswick.)

122. New Prospect, Oklahoma

123. *Prescription: Murder* by Ann Kurth

124. Farrah Fawcett

125. Andy Griffith

126. Ernesta and Gwendolin

127. Caryll Chessman

128. By having Jeff's office repainted with poisoned paint

Cases in History

1. Sir Robert Peel

2. None; Lizzie Borden was found innocent of the slaying of her parents.

3. Approximately 2.7 million dollars in currency, coin, checks, money orders, and securities.

4. Bobby Franks

5. "I've been waiting all night for you." (The myth that he said, "Don't shoot, G-men, don't shoot" was fabricated by J. Edgar Hoover.)

6. Dr. Carl Austin Weiss

7. Vincenzo Peruggia

8. The murder of Mary Cecilia Rogers

9. Bruno Hauptmann

10. The ambush took place at Sears Crossing with the actual robbery taking place at Bridego Bridge near Mentmore, Buckinghamshire, England.

11. Eddie Egan and Sonny Grosso

12. Albert DeSalvo

13. His wife

14. F. Lee Bailey
15. The Whitechapel section
16. Harry K. Thaw
17. Anna Sage
18. Salvatore Maranzano
19. "Murph the Surf"
20. The Clutter Family
21. He had an extra Y chromosome
22. Caril Fugate; fourteen
23. He had a heart attack while in prison at the age of sixty-seven.
24. William Kemmler on August 6, 1890, at Auburn prison.
25. In a coffinlike wooden box buried eighteen-inches underground.

The Murder of the Basking Family

1. "The Poisoned Chocolate Case" by Anthony Berkely
2. *Shroud for a Nightingale* by P. D. James
3. *The Genuine Article* by A. B. Guthrie
4. "A Taste for Honey" by Gerald Heard
5. "The Grey Room" by Eden Phillpotts

6. *Unnatural Death* by Dorothy Sayers

7. "The Mystery of the Speckled Band" by Sir Arthur Conan Doyle

8. *Goldfinger* by Ian Fleming

9. "The Murders in Rue Morgue" by Edgar Allan Poe.

10. *Overture to Death* by Ngaio Marsh

The murderer turned out to be county medical man Dr. Jim Pastor (Pastor is another word for Shepherd (Sheppard)—*The Murder of Roger Achroyd* by Agatha Christie).

The Masters' Quiz...
For Experts Only

1. Proprietor of the Mysterious Bookshop, publisher of the Mysterious Press, and a noted critic, editor, and occasional author.

2 By shortening her father's mother's name Blaisdell

3. 129 West 56th Street, New York City

4. The birth of Sherlock Holmes

5. 137596

6. His Father Christmas beard

7. Pam and Jerry North

8. He majored in psychology for one year at the

University of Hawaii and then transfered to Berkeley where he completed his last three years majoring in police science.

9. Best first mystery short story of the year

10. A nonfiction work by P. D. James with Thomas A. Critchley concerning England's Radcliffe's Highway Murders of 1811.